Leading
Insights

Biblical Worldview and Spiritual Formation

Printed in the United States of America

28 27 26 25 24 23   1 2 3 4 5 6

Edited by Swaner, Lynn E.

ACSI Leading Insights: Biblical Worldview and Spiritual Formation

ISBN 978-1-58331-523-1

eISBN 978-1-58331-524-8

Catalog#: 6682
          e6682

Designers: Patrick Flowers
           Caitlyn Scannell

Cover design: Lisa Ruppert
              Jeff Barnes

Association of Christian Schools International
PO Box 62249 • Colorado Springs, CO 80962
Care Team: 800.367.0798 • www.acsi.org

CONTENTS

Introduction
Lynn E. Swaner, *Series Editor*

In their global research on today's teenagers, Barna (2022) found this generation to display a remarkable openness to Jesus and the Bible, along with a generally positive view of both. At the same time, the research identified a considerable gap between the percentage of teens who identify as Christians and those who say they have made a personal commitment to follow Jesus. And even among teens who regularly engage with the Bible, many do not endorse the tenets of orthodox Christian faith or see the Bible as meaningfully informing their lives.

When it comes to closing the gap between teens' openness and their commitment to a vibrant faith, there is good news: teens cite adults—whether parents, mentors, teachers, or youth pastors—as the primary source of mentorship and guidance in their faith development. The research concludes that to "bring this open generation to a place of deeper understanding and reliance upon the word of God will take a village" (Barna Group 2022, 14). Christian schools play an important role in this village square, not just for teens, but for children of all ages—importantly, the research "hints at the urgency and intentionality needed to plant young people in God's word as early as possible" (29–31).

To this end, rather than a sprinkling of scriptures, doctrine, or spiritual practices, Christian schools seek to offer an education woven from the very fabric of their faith commitments (Hughes and Adrian 1997, 1). Biblical worldview development and spiritual formation, for both students and faculty, often lie at the heart of this effort. This monograph explores the ways Christian educators frame these concepts and consequently shape their pedagogy, curricula, and professional development in light of them.

Creating a Framework

Crucial to schools' biblical worldview development and spiritual formation efforts is the creation of "a philosophical framework that accounts for the unrestricted interplay between faith and learning as implied by our vision statements" (Hull 2003, 212). There is consensus that such a framework should be Bible-based and Christo-centric, with both individual goals for student and faculty growth as well as corporate goals for cultivating Christian community (Graham 2003, 205). However, there are diverse approaches to biblical worldview and spiritual formation in Christian schools which, though sometimes a question of semantics, can also result from influences like varying denominational theologies, emphases on particular spiritual practices, and interpretations of enlightenment thought (to name a few).

Put simply, there are no quick shortcuts to creating a framework for biblical worldview and spiritual formation. Schools and educators need to do the hard work of developing such a framework—with biblical faithfulness as the *sine qua non*—that is appropriate to their own contexts. This monograph is intended to help educators in doing so, with particular attention given in the first section, *Philosophy and Research*, to developing frameworks for biblical worldview and spiritual formation in Christian schools.

Moving Toward Practice

Importantly, this monograph was written by practitioners, for practitioners; thus, the second and third sections—*Christian School Perspectives* and *Programs and Practices*—are written with an eye toward developing coherent practice in classrooms and schools. In the second section, authors share from the perspectives of school leadership, classroom instruction, curricular development, and faculty training. In the third, authors share specific programs and approaches that have proved effective in the Christian school setting.

Across these chapters, readers will discern the need for a collective approach to biblical worldview development and spiritual formation in Christian schools. In other words, aligning philosophy to practice is not the work of a single individual or sole department. Instead, schools are in need of three things:

- *Shared language*—An essential component of any framework for practice must include a common language that is known and used by school leaders, teachers, students, and families. This should include definitions of key terms (like biblical worldview and spiritual formation), clear signposting of these terms in the school's core documents, and regular use in communication to all constituents. Shared language is the starting point for developing coherent practice together and is essential for determining and assessing the effectiveness of that practice.

- *Shared practices*—These are the approaches and strategies that are collectively developed and implemented throughout the school, with consistency and fidelity to the school's philosophical framework. While this includes direct instruction on biblical worldview and spiritual formation, it also includes integrative framing and scaffolding of learning and development activities with a view to the same. Moreover, ACSI's Flourishing Schools Research (Swaner, Marshall, and Tesar 2019) also identified the importance of applying knowledge through action; when present at a given school, constructs like community engagement, serving students with disabilities, and teachers' best practice orientation are linked with higher rates of alumni reporting they are walking with God. While correlational and not causal, these findings suggest the need for students and faculty alike to have facilitated opportunities at school to "live out" the Gospel, by loving their neighbors, caring well for those with special needs, and striving for excellence in all they do (Colossians 3:23).

- *Shared time*—Nothing worth doing in schools is accomplished without shared time-on-task, in terms of both number of hours and regular engagement across the school year (or, more accurately, years). Developing a shared language and practices for biblical worldview and spiritual formation is not a one-and-done affair— just like growing in love, knowledge, and understanding as part of discipleship is a "more and more" proposition (Philippians 1:9–11). In truth, "Whatever we write down in our mission statements … how we invest our time and money is often an accurate reflection of what we actually believe as individuals and organizations" (Swaner and Wolfe 2021, 171). The investment of school resources, including precious instructional and professional development time, should match the degree to which biblical worldview development and spiritual formation are central to the school's mission.

Although school approaches will differ in structure and format, these three factors—shared language, practices, and time—are essential to bringing a school's framework for biblical worldview development and spiritual formation to life, for both students and faculty.

Reflection and Action

Research shows that professional practice is most effectively transformed when adults engage in a cycle of reflection and action (Swaner 2016). In other words, educators need to reflect on what they have learned and strategize for intentionally putting that learning into practice. To this end, this monograph includes a final section that features a set of reflection questions on the relationship between the school's philosophy, policy, curricular development, pedagogy, and constituent relationships with its approach to biblical worldview development and spiritual formation. Consider reading this monograph and engaging in these questions together with colleagues, either informally or through a book study.

In his letter to the Colossian church, the apostle Paul urges believers to let "the word of Christ dwell in you richly, teaching and admonishing one another in all wisdom, singing psalms and hymns and spiritual songs, with thankfulness in your hearts to God" (Colossians 3:16). When Christian schools intentionally craft their philosophy and practice for biblical worldview development and spiritual formation, they can better invite students and faculty alike into the richness of God's Word, a deeper walk with Christ, and the beauty of Christian community. Regardless of the specific terms used, there is hardly a Christian school mission that would not resonate with these Kingdom aims. May you be abundantly blessed in your pursuit of them.

Part 1:
Philosophy and Research

Biblical Worldview and Spiritual Formation: Frameworks and Definitions
Jerry Nelson, *ACSI*

Our worldview is an inescapable reality that colors everything we communicate. We are the products of where we are born and raised, by whom we were raised, how we were nurtured, our collection of experiences (for better or worse), and how these experiences shaped our temperaments. In other words, we bring an inescapable bias to the table that is a product of how the Lord crafted us and the time and place in which He chose for us to be born. Ultimately, the collection of ideas and understandings about our reality constitutes our worldview. And this worldview is a narrative that influences how we think, how we interpret things, and ultimately what we believe to be truth. This is true of every human being who has ever lived.

Yet there is still a more powerful factor that shapes our worldview. In Numbers 13, the Lord commands Moses to send out spies to explore the land He had promised to give them. Twelve leaders were chosen from each tribe for the reconnaissance expedition. After being sent out and spending forty days in the land gathering evidence Moses requested, they concluded that the land was indeed flowing with milk and honey. There was no dispute about what the land possessed and who possessed the land. Yet the twelve produced two different reports—two different interpretations of the experience. Same data, same evidence, two interpretations reflecting different understandings of reality. How is this so? What factor accounts for two varying interpretations? The difference maker was the condition of their hearts.

In this chapter, we will explore the question of "what is a worldview?" We will survey both God's Word and key theologians and philosophers as we frame out an answer to this question. Because there are different kinds of worldviews, we'll also examine what defines a *biblical* worldview, which is the worldview that Christian schools seek to develop in students. Finally, we will explore the ways in which the condition of the human heart fundamentally shapes not only the development but also the living out of a biblical worldview—thereby drawing necessary connections between worldview development and spiritual formation.

What Is a Worldview?

A worldview is a collection of presuppositions, examined or unexamined, that inform a person's view of reality. It has been described as a filter or a lens through which an individual interprets the world; how one conceptualizes reality; the representation of one's total outlook on life; the mind's desire to seek unity amid great diversity; or a set of beliefs about the most important issues of life. While worldviews are difficult to discern in a holistic way, they can be understood along three different poles: a person's view of God, view of humankind, and view of truth.

If there is a consensus among theologians and philosophers, it is the idea that a worldview is the formation of a mental picture about reality and this mental picture manifests itself in a story. It is a story we tell about ourselves and the world around us—a narrative, communally absorbed and individually apprehended. Perhaps the most comprehensive definition of a worldview has been provided by David Naugle (2005) in *Worldview: The History of a Concept:*

> [Worldview is] a semiotic system of narrative signs that creates the definitive symbolic universe which is responsible in the main for the shape of a variety of life-determining, human practices. It creates the channels in which the waters of reason flow. It establishes the horizons of an interpreter's point of view by which texts of all types are understood. It is that mental medium by which the world is known. The human heart is its home, and it provides a home for the human heart. (330)

Naugle notes that the concept of a *worldview* is relatively new in the history of ideas. The first noted appearance of worldview or *Weltanschauung* is in Immanuel Kant's *Critique of Judgement*, according to James Orr, it was largely used as a technical term "denoting the widest view which the mind can take of things in the effort to grasp them together as a whole from the standpoint of some particular philosophy or theology" (Naugle 2005, 7, 58). Kant's philosophical thought was instrumental in effectively severing scientific thought from its religious basis. It ushered in a wave of hypercriticism of all religious or superstitious presuppositions. This has contributed to the ever-present secular-sacred divide.

This was indeed a revolution, given that the primary assumption held in Europe at the time was that God is the center and the ultimate determiner of reality (Hoffecker and Currid 2007). Although the concept of a world-view was prevalent amongst German thinkers, it was largely concentrated in academic philosophical circles. It was not until it began to make its way into the natural science, and more prominently in the social sciences (notably Sigmund Freud and Karl Marx), that the threat to Christianity was most prominently felt. This new understanding of reality produced by the Enlightenment thinkers ultimately led to a crisis in Christian thought.

As such, it was necessary for Christian thinkers who encountered these philosophical challenges to answer them in a credible way, which required immersion in the world of philosophical discourse. What emerged was a group of Christian thinkers who began to conceive of Christianity as a comprehensive worldview, in its own right, to demonstrate that it met all the challenges levied against it. Naugle (2005) is quick to note that *Weltanschauung* carries with it philosophical baggage since its emergence did not originate from God's Word, and as such it must be examined for its "illicit content" and replaced with "licit content" (289); in other words, Naugle believes *Weltanschauung* can be redeemed and adopted as a concept to meet the philosophical challenges of our day.

Defining a Biblical Worldview

The development of a Christian *Weltanschauung*, or conceiving Christianity as a worldview, did not formally make its way into the English lexicon until its introduction by James Orr. It was then popularized by Abraham Kuyper in his *Stone Lectures*, based on Calvin's Institutes. Philosophers, theologians, and apologists such as Gordon Clark, Carl F.H. Henry, Herman Dooyeweerd, and Francis Schaeffer further developed the concept of a Christian worldview. Christianity as a worldview is robust enough to meet the philosophical challenges brought on by the Enlightenment as well as the social challenges of our post-truth/post-Christian paradigm.

If a worldview is a set of narrative signs that influence how we think, interpret, and categorize knowledge of the world, then a biblical worldview is thinking, interpreting, and knowing, with a heart converted to God with His Word as the final rule in faith and practice (Williamson 2004). So, then, what narrative signs do the scriptures clearly communicate? The biblical narrative has been expressed in four acts, movements, or epochs: Creation, Fall, Redemption, and Restoration (Plantinga 2002).

- **Creation:** In the beginning, God created the heavens and the earth. God created people in His own image. God saw all that He had made, and it was good (Genesis 1). As image bearers we are personal (we have deep longings), rational (we have understanding), volitional (we are able to make choices), and emotional (we have feelings) (Crabb 1987). There are implications for bearing God's image. Those include caring for creation, using our creativity, communing with others, conforming to the image of Christ (through renewing our mind), and contemplating the goodness and glory of God, His creation and activity within it (Plantinga 2002).

- **Fall:** We were created for wholeness, for harmony, for perfect fellowship with God. But our self-centeredness and desire for autonomy—essentially our rebellion—dissolved the fabric of that fellowship (Genesis 3). Sin breached the relationship between God and humanity. When this relationship was broken, it uncoupled every relationship connected to it: people with people (wars, murder, discrimination, prejudice), man with woman (divorce, abuse, broken families), people with nature (alienation, pollution, species extinction), and people with themselves (guilt, shame, fear).

- **Redemption:** Deep down we long for renewal, for redemption. Jesus—God incarnate—lived a perfect, sinless life and died on a cross to pay the penalty for our sin. And, three days later, He rose from the dead, demonstrating His power to rescue us and our world from sin, death, and brokenness. Only He can give us true freedom and mend our relationships with God, others, ourselves, and all of creation. Redemption is found through faith in Christ alone, by grace alone (Colossians 1:13–14; Ephesians 2:8–9).

- **Restoration:** The Bible paints a very bright picture of the future for the people of God. All God's children will be restored into perfect relationships—people with people, people with themselves, people with creation and most importantly, people with God: the Creator, Redeemer, and Restorer (Revelation 21). Until this time, believers are to engage the world as Christ's ambassadors, through sharing the gospel, loving their neighbors, and doing the good works that God has appointed (2 Corinthians 5:20, Matthew 28:16–20, Matthew 22:36–40, Ephesians 2:10).

While a key component to the biblical worldview is this narrative, there are also philosophical, theological, apologetic, and ethical factors to consider in its development. I will suggest some key questions to consider in the development of a robust biblical worldview for each.

Philosophy

J.P. Moreland and William Lane Craig, in *Philosophical Foundations for a Christian Worldview*, write that philosophy is "the most foundational of all other disciplines, since it examines the presuppositions and ramifications of every discipline …" (n.d. 2017, 3). They define philosophy as "the attempt to think rationally and critically about life's most important questions in order to obtain knowledge and wisdom about them" and assert that "philosophy can help someone form a rationally justified, true worldview" (3). This has been critical over the last two hundred years as Christianity has most often been attacked on the grounds of its underlying presuppositions. The biblical worldview passes, comprehensively and coherently, any and all philosophical tests (Nash 2010). A sound philosophical foundation is necessary for a sound ethic. Key questions in developing a sound philosophical foundation are:

- What is ultimate reality?
- What is good?
- What is of value?
- What is beautiful?
- What is truth?
- How do we know what we know?

Theology

Medieval educators believed that the study of philosophy was necessary to effectively engage in theology. Philosophy aids theology in at least two ways: it provides a foundation for interpreting and systematizing scripture, and it aids theology in the task of integrating God's Word into every aspect of life (Moreland and Craig n.d. 2017). With about 75 percent of scripture being in some form of narrative or poetry (BibleProject 2023), moral truths must be extracted and organized to present a unified testimony of God's nature, activity, and purpose for creation. Systematic theology (or Bible doctrine) is the discipline of organizing these truths in an accessible way. It is particularly helpful for those who are young in their faith development to having some basic truths to hold on to as they navigate through scripture.

It goes without saying that knowing God's Word is at the core of a biblical worldview. While there are many doctrinal categories by which to organize the revelation of God (i.e. soteriology, eschatology, ecclesiology, pneumatology), all teachings should be framed within the history of salvation. Key questions in developing a sound doctrinal formation are:

- What does scripture say about the purpose/significance of God revealing Himself to humankind?
- What does scripture say about the intent of this revelation being codified in the Holy scripture?
- What does scripture say about who God is? What is His nature? What has He revealed?

- What does scripture say about what it means to be human? What is our responsibility to God? What is our responsibility to creation?
- What does scripture say about what can be known? What is truth? What is the ultimate source of knowledge? What is our responsibility with knowledge and truth?

Apologetics

The discipline that deals with the rational defense of the Christian faith is known as apologetics. It is aided by both philosophy and theology. Philosophy provides the tools for developing a reasonable response, and theology provides the systematized content to facilitate a response. Apologetics is concerned with answering those who criticize the historicity, authenticity, and coherence of scripture. It is not that scripture needs human affirmation to be true; however, we are commanded to give a reason for the hope that is in us (1 Peter 3:15). We are also commanded to love God with all our heart, soul, and mind. As Norman Geisler and Thomas Howe (2004) note in *When Critics Ask*, "Part of our loving duty to Christ is to find answers for those who criticize God's Word" (9).

Apologetics involves the development of a framework for analyzing all worldviews against a biblical worldview. It also may include processing life experiences (specifically those that negatively impact us) in light of the truths in God's Word about His sovereignty and providence. Apologetics done rightly should contribute to greater assurance of salvation in Jesus Christ. Key questions that arise in apologetics include those related to:

- The scriptures; for example, is the Bible a reliable source?
- The Incarnation; for example, is Jesus Christ the Son of God?
- The Resurrection; or, did Jesus Christ truly rise from the dead?
- The problem of evil; for example, if God is good why is there so much evil in the world? Why do bad things happen to good people?

Ethics

Paul says in 2 Corinthians 5:14–15, "For the love of Christ controls us, because we have concluded this: that one has died for all." For Paul, it was the knowledge of God that spurred him on as a minister of reconciliation. James 2:14 asks the question, "What good is it, my brothers, if someone says he has faith but does not have works?" In Mark 10:45, Jesus defined what it means to be great in the kingdom of God—servanthood. In scripture, there is a clear call to action. What we "ought" to do is clear.

The study of ethics (also known as moral philosophy or moral theory) is the study of what we "ought" to do. It is concerned with the rightness and wrongness of human conduct. The study of ethics assumes objectivity— there is a standard on which to judge human conduct. This standard rests outside of humankind. As such, Christian ethics is morality founded on, framed, and informed by the Word of God. While scripture doesn't speak specifically to every issue, it is nonetheless the final rule in faith and practice, superintending every thought and action of a follower of Christ. Christian ethics is the outward manifestation of a sound biblical worldview. True Christian ethics is action that exhibits Christlikeness. Key questions that can frame a biblical view of ethics are:

- What does the Bible clearly state to be right and wrong?
- How do we determine right and wrong regarding a situation for which there is no specific command in scripture?
- What pattern of "right living" does the Bible set forth?
- What does it mean to live faithfully according to the pattern of Christ in our present moment?
- What should be the Christian's disposition about culture (the *zeitgeist* or the spirit of the age)?

The categories above are suggestive of a spiritual trellis on which a believer's faith can grow. However, it is important to note that the study of philosophy, theology, apologetics, or ethics in a formal sense is not necessary for faith in Christ. The thief on the cross was not given a systematic theology test to gain entrance into heaven. Naugle (2005) offers wise caution:

[I]t is also possible for Christian worldview advocates to cultivate an immoderate enthusiasm for their biblical systems with their cultural and apologetic potential and to become forgetful of the God who stands behind them. It is a grave mistake to confuse or substitute a proper relationship with the trinitarian God for the crafting and promulgation of a Christian *Weltanschauung* .... A rightly ordered love both divine and human ought to be the ultimate outcome of all our actions, including that of biblical worldview development .... It would be a mistake, however, to so focus on the coherent organization of such propositions as to neglect the personal God they present. No systematic, biblical *Weltanschauung* ought to usurp the primacy of Truth and the ultimate end of agapic love. (338)

It is to the question of "rightly ordered love"—or the relationship between biblical worldview and spiritual formation—that we now turn.

The Condition of the Heart

The Israelites' exodus from Egypt provides for us one of the earliest case studies of worldview development (Hoffecker and Currid 2007). In fact, the episode of the twelve spies' reports helps shine light on Naugle's definition. Consider what the Lord says to Moses concerning the bad report: "How long will these people treat me with contempt? How long will they refuse to believe in me, in spite of all the signs I have performed among them?" (Numbers 14:11, NIV).

Two questions emerge from this: what were the signs God performed among them? And what was God's purpose in producing the signs? The ten plagues, the parting of the Red Sea, the pillar of cloud by day and fire by night, the manna and occasional quail, water from the rock, hearing the voice of God, and the other miraculous interventions in the wilderness storyline all were meant to communicate to these former captives that the Lord is God, that He is one, and that He chose Israel to be His conduit of salvation for mankind. The issuing of the Ten Commandments—outlining

17

the standard for people's relationship to God and their relationship to each other—pointed to and painted a narrative of God's providential and sovereign rulership. This grand narrative of God's activity in His creation and relationship with His special creation—human beings—effectively formed the foundation for the rest of the scriptural narrative.

The power of these narrative-forming signs and wonders performed by God was that it served to cleanse the Israelites of four hundred years of immersion in Egyptian cultural and correct their understanding of reality. Hoffecker calls this one of the earliest "Revolutions in Worldview." To codify these signs and wonders for all eternity, the Lord directs Moses, by the Holy Spirit, to record them. The Torah codifies the Israelites' view of God (triune, infinite, personal), human beings (made in the image of God, fully dignified, fallen, redeemable), the ultimate source of truth (revelation by God for salvation, and through nature by discovery), and the purpose of creation (to bring glory to God). It would provide the framework for which they would think, interpret, and understand the world around them. It provided them with a worldview centered on God and their relationship with Him.

Each of the twelve spies had access to this information—seeing the miracles with their own eyes, knowing the story of their origin and their unique place in history—yet they did not view things the same. This story, and others throughout scripture, provides a clear understanding of the core factor determining a worldview—the condition of the heart. Generally speaking, there are only two conditions of the heart, as Naugle (2005) asserts: "a heart converted to God or a heart averted to God" (26). Either the heart is a slave to righteousness or a slave to sin (Romans 6:15–23). As Naugle notes, "The diversity and relativity of worldviews, therefore, must be traced to the idolatry and the noetic effects of sin upon the human heart" (276). Those hearts that have not been transformed by the Holy Spirit have been "given over" to the lust and the passions of the flesh (Romans 1:18–25). Therefore, we can conclude that a biblical worldview, in its most basic sense, is a heart that is converted to God's view of Himself, reality, humankind, and truth. This worldview continues to grow in terms of its application in believers' lives, in proportion to the growth in their knowledge of and relationship with Him.

The account of the twelve spies should also serve as a warning to us lest we think we are the prime cause of transformation. God provided the best-possible curriculum for spiritual formation and transformation, yet ten of the twelve did not believe. We must remember that many did not believe Jesus' message after they saw Him perform miracles (Mark 2). We serve God as He calls out those whom He has chosen, but we don't *cause* transformation. That is exclusively the work of the Holy Spirit. The Christian educator's responsibility then is to cultivate the soil to aid the transformation process. This is not an either-or proposition; this is a matter of priority. It is the curriculum behind "teaching them to observe all that I have commanded you" (Matthew 28:18–20).

Biblical worldview development ultimately serves spiritual formation. If a biblical worldview is ultimately a matter of the heart, then the Holy Spirit will manifest itself in a Caleb-like declaration: "We should go up and take possession of the land, for we can certainly do it" (Numbers 13:30, NIV). Caleb's was a heart converted to God with a desire to know God and be vigorously obedient to His will. To our knowledge Caleb didn't have a formal course in philosophy or theology as we understand it today, but he and the Israelites were presented with the signs and symbols that pointed to God's existence and will for His creation. If this is true, then it may be said that the responsibility of the Christian educator is to faithfully present the signs and symbols of the existence, providential care, and sovereign rule of God and to be visible testimonies and representations of Jesus Christ and allow the Holy Spirit to do the rest (2 Corinthians 3:18; Colossians 3:10; Ephesians 4:24).

We can thank God every day for taking our hearts of stone and replacing them with hearts of flesh (Ezekiel 11:14–21). For whatever our circumstances were at the time of birth and whatever they are now, we should see them new and afresh with the mind of Christ (Philippians 2:5). And as Christian educators, we can intentionally equip our students with the tools to deepen and defend their faith, as we tell the story of God's love and faithfulness in the way we live.

Biblical Worldview and Spiritual Formation: Insights from Research
Matt Lee and Eric Price

We know from scripture that the command to nurture the faith of the next generation (Psalm 78:4, 6) is blessed with the promise of flourishing faith (Deuteronomy 6:4–9; Proverbs 9:9; Ephesians 6:4). However, trends in the United States suggest the Christian faith is declining (Barna Group and ACSI 2017; Barna Group 2007; Pew Research Center 2015) while hostility toward faith is increasing (Family Research Council 2017). It has never been more important for Christian schools to understand how to best support students' faith formation.

While research documents that faith can be shaped throughout life (Blos 1967; Wink and Dillon 2002; Kroger 2003; Astin et al. 2004; Braskamp 2007), much research demonstrates that faith is formed in early adolescence (Erickson 1992; Kim-Spoon, Longo, and McCullough 2012; Hardy et al. 2019) and is largely stable thereafter in a "permanent place of equilibrium" (Fowler 1995, 172; Hitlin and Piliavin 2004). This reality underscores the importance of understanding faith and nurturing development during the schooling years.

Empirically speaking, research suggests that parents (see, for example, White and Matawie 2004; Marks 2004; Willits and Crider 1989; Iannaccone 1990; Lee, Rice, and Gillespie 1997; Peterson 2006; Fawcett, Francis, and McKenna 2021), peers (King, Furrow, and Roth 2002; Gunnoe and Moore 2002), and churches (Krispin 2004; Cort 2008; Gantt 2004; Schultz 2012; Haynes 2006; Hembree 2007) play the greatest role in shaping students' faith. However, outside of these influences, Christian primary and secondary schools may play the greatest role (Regnerus, Smith, and Smith 2004; Taylor 2009).

Research identifying distinctive outcomes of Christian school graduates compared to peers in other sectors provides suggestive evidence of the robust role Christian schools play in students' spiritual formation. Graduates of Christian schools are more likely than their public or secular private school peers to seek a vocation that fulfills religious calling (Casagrande, Pennings, and Sikkink 2019); volunteer and participate in charitable causes (Cardus 2019b; Cheng and Iselin 2020); engage in civic life and express prosocial orientation (Pennings, Sikkink, and Berner 2014; Green et al. 2016; Sikkink 2018a); participate actively in their churches (Green et al. 2016; Cardus 2019c); practice spiritual disciplines (Cardus 2019c; Sikkink 2018b); and remain in an intact marriage (Wolf et al. 2022; Schwarz and Sikkink 2017). Together, these findings suggest that Christian schools play a role in influencing a student's faith and practice.

Given that Christian schools desire to nurture spiritual formation in their students, it is important to understand which components of Christian school culture and effectiveness reinforce flourishing faith in the context of the school environment (Drexler and Bagby 2021). In this review of the literature, we focus on four broad categories of Christian school characteristics: leadership, teaching, relationships, and institutional features. We then conclude with considerations for measuring faith formation in Christian schools.

Christian School Characteristics

Leading the Christian School

Establishing a vision for spiritual formation in Christian schools begins with school leadership. Christian school leaders may directly foster an environment for shaping students' faith by providing direction and aligning the school's mission with the Christian faith (Pennings and Wiens 2011; Beckman, Drexler, and Eames 2012; Sikkink 2012; Lee, Cheng, and Wiens 2021). Indeed, ACSI's Flourishing Schools research found that leaders help establish a school's purpose, including integrating a Christian worldview into all aspects of the life of the school (Swaner, Dodds, and Lee 2021). School leaders exercise control over curriculum, personnel decisions, and school resources, as they shape school culture and thereby indirectly influence the spiritual formation of students. Through these key decisions, Christian school leaders may hire staff members who will help promote the school mission (Russo 2009; Murray 2011; Beckman, Drexler, and Eames 2012).

Christian school leaders may also promote a particular vision for Christian education that is more conducive to spiritual formation (Hunter 2008). According to one study using a nationally representative sample of U.S. school leaders, the majority of Protestant school principals emphasize college preparation or personal growth as the top educational goal for their school, and are significantly less likely to emphasize academic achievement or vocational preparation than public school administrators (Lee 2021). Further, leaders of faith-based schools prepare for their leadership roles differently relative to their peers in other sectors, perhaps signaling the differentiated priorities and expectations of faith-based education (Lee and Cheng 2021). A survey of leaders of Council on Educational Standards and Accountability member schools finds that these particular school leaders prioritize fostering religious or spiritual development as one of the top two educational goals for their school (Lee, Cheng, and Wiens 2021). One qualitative study of six Christian school administrators similarly finds that these leaders believe an important part of the leader's role is to preserve missional fidelity (Harrison 2012). These findings are consistent with scholarly claims that faith-based education must emphasize moral education and the development of virtue alongside academic excellence (Wynne and Walberg 1985; DeHaan et al. 1997).

Christian school leaders may also directly shape students' faith through their example of lived faith (Beckman, Drexler, and Eames 2012). For example, in a survey of Protestant and Catholic school leaders in the U.S. and Canada, Sikkink (2012) finds that Protestant school leaders are more likely to view themselves as a spiritual role model to students than their Catholic school peers. A qualitative study of twelve Christian school leaders confirms the importance of spiritual leadership to these leaders, who articulated the importance of personal practices and relationships with others (Banke, Maldonado, and Lacey 2012). Another qualitative study of six Christian school leaders similarly finds that these leaders believed it was important for them to embody servant leadership (Harrison 2012). Research conducted in Christian higher education institutions finds similar emphasis on spiritual leadership (Burch, Swails, and Mills 2015).

Finally, many Christian school leaders are responsible for hiring teachers who profess the Christian faith. In a recent study, Christian school leaders indicated they would be unwilling to give up their right to "hire on mission" in order to participate in a private school choice program (Lee, Price, and Swaner 2022). Beyond just a profession of faith, however, teachers in Christian schools pursue distinctive educational practices to integrate faith and learning (Smith and Smith 2011; Cheng 2018)—which leads to the next characteristic of Christian schools that promote faith formation.

Teaching in Christian Schools

Of course, spiritual formation in Christian schools cannot be considered apart from the adults with whom students predominantly interact—their teachers. Graduates of evangelical Protestant schools are more likely to report a positive, caring relationship with their teachers than public school graduates (Cardus 2019a). Christian school teachers may embody or cultivate spiritual practices that deepen students' faith. As Smith and Smith write, "Christian practices can contribute to how teaching and learning are carried out and experienced" (2011, 11).

Integration of Faith and Learning

As the school staff who primarily interact with students, teachers play a key role in their spiritual formation (Holloway et al. 2019). The intersection of spiritual formation and teaching practices is often described as the integration of faith and learning. According to Smith and Smith (2011), this integration is something that "called into question the very idea of 'secular' or 'neutral' learning, emphasized a faith-inspired affirmation of intellectual pursuits and refused to settle for models that positioned faith and learning as merely complementary or parallel" (2). Kanitz (2005) argues that a robust integration of faith and learning should consider not only shared core beliefs, but also distinctions across denominations and theological traditions (Romans 14:5). Similarly, Cooling (2005) advocates for developing theological curiosity and contextualization in teachers. Faith-based education is most robust when teachers are firmly rooted in their faith.

How well do Christian school teachers integrate faith into their pedagogy and classroom instruction? While there is disagreement on how best to integrate faith and learning (Acree 1994), one survey of primary and secondary Christian school teachers finds that teachers express high levels of confidence with respect to the integration of faith and learning, and that, unsurprisingly, Bible teachers express higher levels of self-efficacy and integrate the Bible more frequently than all other content areas (Williams 2021). Worldview may also vary with teaching experience, with more experienced teachers expressing higher levels of worldview as measured by the Worldview Assessment Instrument and Credal Statements (Evans 2015), particularly with experienced Bible teachers (Fyock 2008). Worldview integration may also vary across schooling contexts. Comparative studies of Association of Christian Schools International (ACSI) member schools and Association of Classical Christian Schools (ACCS) member schools noted that while schools in both organizations emphasized biblical worldview, they nonetheless exhibited key differences, including teaching methods (e.g., the *trivium*), accreditation (Peterson 2012), and the expressed worldview of teachers (Wood 2008). Another study, while not examining the integration of faith and teaching per se, documented evidence that science teachers in Christian schools emphasize curricular content in distinctive ways relative to peers in public schools (Cheng 2018). At the very least, education founded upon the tenets of Christianity should appear inconsistent with teaching in secular contexts (Smith 2009).

Over time, Christian school students may grow in alignment with their teachers' faith. A descriptive study using the Raymond Meyer Worldview Instrument to measure worldview in Christian school students found evidence that students enrolled in a Christian school hold to a strong biblical position, though the study lacked a comparison group (Meyer 2003). A longitudinal study of one Christian school found that mean differences between student and faculty worldview scores as measured by the Politics, Economics, Education, Religion, and Social Issues (PEERS) test decreased over time, suggesting that students became more like teachers with respect to worldview (Fyock 2008). In a comparative study using the

Meyer instrument, Taylor (2009) found evidence of differences in worldview between public school students and those who had received worldview training for seven or more years at a Christian school. Another comparative study of adolescents found that students attending a private Christian school reported significantly higher worldview scores than peers in other school settings (Perkins 2007). Uecker (2008) examined the religious lives of adolescents in different schooling contexts and Christian traditions and found Protestant schooling to be associated with greater salience of faith in later life. A study of a representative sample of American high school graduates found an evangelical Protestant school advantage with respect to graduates continuing in religious practices and beliefs (Pennings, Sikkink, and Berner 2014). At a policy level, the abolition of compulsory religious schooling in Germany led to lower levels of adult religiosity at the national level (Arold, Woessmann, and Zierow 2022). These studies lend credence to the idea that teachers may help nurture a biblical worldview, strengthening the case for Christian education while simultaneously justifying Christian parents' concerns over secular education.

A small number of studies cast doubt on the efficacy of Christian education to foster worldview formation. In contrast to Meyer, Taylor, Perkins, Uecker, and Pennings et al., one study compared students' biblical worldview and failed to detect significant differences by Christian school attendance (Baniszewski 2016). Similarly, in a higher education context, Simoneaux (2015) compared biblical worldviews of Apostolic Pentecostal students attending Apostolic Christian colleges with those of the same faith tradition attending secular colleges and found no evidence of meaningful differences.

Courses and Content

Courses and content may also play a formational role. Curriculum must be aligned with the school's mission, purpose, and the objectives of educational completion and attainment, as well as make use of literature that supports a school's moral aims (MacIntyre 2007; Drexler and Bagby 2021).

Many Christian schools offer or require coursework in Bible, worldview, or apologetics. Previous research has examined the relationship between biblical worldview curricula and interventions on students' worldview, with inconclusive results. Two studies find evidence suggesting a positive relationship. A causal/comparative study of the *Understanding the Times* worldview course surveyed a random sample of Christian high school students across the United States at various times and found a positive relationship between the course and students' worldview (Barrows 2014). A study of a biblical worldview intervention in a hybrid mode of education context in California charter schools found the intervention increased students' worldview as measured by the PEERS test (Barke 2014).

Other studies fail to find evidence of a relationship between worldview curricula and students' biblical worldview. A pre-post study of an exposition and exegesis course for eleventh-and twelfth-grade students at one Christian school found that while students who acknowledged their Christian faith were more likely to score higher on the posttest measuring worldview, the course itself did not necessarily increase worldview scores (Brinkley 2021). A study of a Bible curriculum in another Christian high school found no evidence of statistically significant differences in worldview after students had taken the course (Bryant 2008).

Why were some interventions positively associated with worldview while others were not? Two qualitative studies identify features of biblical worldview curricula and interventions that may mediate the relationship between intervention and outcome. According to Mooney (2018), effective biblical worldview programs should have four features: intentional design, personal responsibility, opportunities for application, and intrinsic development. Baley (2021) posits that biblical worldview courses may influence worldview by connecting biblical knowledge with ethical and cultural issues.

One way in which students may learn the "pattern of the sound words" of faith is through catechesis (2 Timothy 1:13; cf. 2 Timothy 1:5, 3:15–17). Gantt (2004) explored the historical and contemporary use of catechism among Protestant denominations from the time of the Protestant Reformation to the establishment of modern denominations, and into the 21st century, and found that "the proponents of catechetical instruction saw it as passing the truth from one generation to another" (187). The use of formal catechism among students of various denominations of Christian faith has been in decline since the 20th century, and Gantt notes that there does seem to be a role for formal conveyance of Christian beliefs to students today, catechetical or otherwise. In contrast, Cooling (2005) argues for preferential use of theological contextualization over replication noting that, while both instructional models must promote scriptural faithfulness, contextualization is preferred due to promotion of theological curiosity.

Other research examines how science coursework may relate to students' worldview. One study used the PEERS assessment to study the worldview of high school students and found students' views towards creationism and evolution tend to be strongly correlated with other elements of biblical worldview (Ray 2001). Two studies of a creationism course at Liberty University found that students were more likely to express views consistent with a creationist worldview as measured by the Creation Worldview Test (Deckard and Sobko 1998) after taking the apologetics course than before the course (Deckard, Henderson, and Grant 2002; Henderson, Deckard, and DeWitt 2003). Given the correlation between the two, if views on creationism and evolution are malleable, biblical worldview may be malleable as well.

Relationships

Education is a process that is affected by relationships (Drexler 2007). Strong relationships and striving after mercy, justice, and faithfulness are found to contribute in meaningful and impactful ways to both faith formation and learning processes (Spears 2005).

School–Family

The partnership between a Christian school and the student's family may be one of the most important relationships with respect to spiritual formation (King, Furrow, and Roth 2002). Several studies documenting the influence of the Christian school on worldview development have commented on the importance of the coherence between school and family as a possible mediator for students' spiritual growth (Uecker 2008). Similarly, Van Meter (2009) argued that while both the Christian school and the family may help shape high school students' worldviews, the family plays the primary role. Perkins (2007) finds a significant relationship between family discipleship and worldview, and identified "the frequency and nature of spiritual discussion, quality of communication in family relationships, family rituals and routines, and the priority of family time" (6) as the channels of influence on adolescents' biblical worldview.

Student–Student

Research documents compelling evidence that peer influence is a significant predictor of faith formation (King, Furrow, and Roth 2002; Regnerus, Smith, and Smith 2004; Schwartz 2006; Cort 2008) and may be a channel by which parental influence on faith is mediated (Martin, White, and Perlman 2003). In particular, perceived support from peers was a significant mediator that was positively associated with church attendance or youth group participation (Schwartz 2006; Cort 2008).

Teacher–Teacher

Discipleship in Christian education is modeled among faculty members professionally through the development of mentoring relationships. Professional development occurs through deliberate support and guidance, both for graduate students aspiring to become teaching professionals and for newer teaching faculty, where more experienced teachers serve as patterns for replication, role models, and conveyers of institutional knowledge to students and young instructional practitioners—underscoring the importance of intentional discipleship within a Christian educational context (Cunningham 2012).

School–Church

One study used the Raymond Meyer Worldview Instrument (Meyer 2003) to measure differences in worldview between Christian school students and their public school peers (Taylor 2009). Evidence of statistically significant differences was found for students who had attended Christian school for seven or more years, suggesting that continually reinforcing integration of biblical truth into instructional and curriculum components may impact the students' worldview. Taylor concluded by arguing that the synergy between church and school may dynamically reinforce faith formation for students. This observation is consistent with other research that finds that students' religious affiliations outside of school predict religious maturity (Ali 2014).

Parent–Child

Parents, as the first and primary influencers, play a key role in the critical early stages of child development. Parental religiosity, especially homogamous religiosity (that is, when both parents share the faith), is linked with prosocial behavior in children (Bartkowski, Xu, and Levin 2008). Parental religiosity is predictive of adult emerging religiosity, particularly when household homogamy (Leonard et al. 2013) and faith support (Leonard et al. 2013; Schwartz 2006) were present. According to Smith (2009), children are content to follow their parents' religious footsteps. One literature review found that children are more likely to share their parents' denomination than they are to share their parents' occupation (Iannaccone 1990). But faith can also undermine young adult religiosity when it is perceived as a source of conflict (Leonard et al. 2013). Taken together, these findings suggest that parents may influence faith formation in children beginning from an early age (Yust 2004).

What are the channels through which a parent may influence a child's faith? One study finds that family spiritual disciplines, including prayer, Bible reading, singing sacred music, and religious service attendance, play an important role (Marks 2004). Students in families who collectively engage in these "family worship" practices scored higher on the Active Faith, and lower on the Materialism/Legalism and Alcoholism/Drug Use, scales (Lee, Rice, and Gillespie 1997). Parents may also influence faith through conversation (Boyatzis and Janicki 2003). Given the important role parents play, Christian schools may consider ways of encouraging active parental involvement in their children's education (Fawcett, Francis, and McKenna 2021; 2022).

School Institutional Features

The institutional features of a school is another important consideration (Volkwein 2010). An analysis of first-year higher education students using data from the 2004 National Survey of Student Engagement (NSSE) finds evidence of differences in spiritual growth by school denominational affiliation, as well as whether the school required chapel, hired only faculty who adhered to the faith, and other institutional characteristics (Lovik 2010). Similarly, in a higher education context, Hill (2009) found that religious participation declined more quickly in Catholic and mainline Protestant university students than in evangelical or secular university students. Theological alignment may have benefits for student achievement as well. Pakaluk (2021) finds student learning to be greatest in schools where students and school are most closely aligned in terms of doctrinal convictions.

School culture is another factor that may influence how effectively a Christian school is able to nurture flourishing faith. ACSI's work on flourishing school culture has uncovered many important relationships between school culture and students' spiritual flourishing (Swaner, Marshall, and Tesar 2019). Mills (2003) posits that the ideal culture for a Christian school is one that is dynamic, interdependent, and service-oriented with a Christ-centered vision. Saphier and King (1985) taxonomize school culture into twelve specific characteristics. Half of these characteristics could be described as representing some aspect of relationships in Christian schools, while others may portray academics, growth, or some other aspect of Christian school culture.

A school's culture extends beyond the classroom to its community and extracurricular activities. A primary marker for distinction of Christian schools is the expectation that teachers embrace their true identity as God's image bearers and therefore reflect God's character through holistic integration of instruction, speech, and action (Graham 2003). Co-curricula can mutually reinforce Christian principles, learning, and learning objectives through school and peer relationships, which extends to school events, traditions, and student life. In this way, community can extend beyond the role of interpersonal relationships to the intentional design of hospitable, welcoming work-life spaces.

Measuring Faith Formation

The fact that "faith is the assurance of things hoped for, the conviction of things not seen" (Hebrews 11:1) implies that there are dimensions of faith that cannot be measured and others that can be measured. Thus, many studies have relied on extrinsic measures of faith as the evidence of things unseen (Hebrews 11:1). If faith is known by deeds (Matthew 7:16; James 2:18), then perhaps faith can be measured indirectly by outward demonstrations that can be measured directly. Here, we highlight several categories of outcomes that have been used to attempt to measure faith formation.

Worldview

Students' knowledge of the Bible (Huber and Huber 2012), the Christian faith (Baley 2021), or doctrinal orthodoxy within a particular theological tradition has been measured in schools. Prior research has documented ways in which students' knowledge and worldview may be linked (Henderson, Deckard, and DeWitt 2003; Pakaluk 2021). While a bevy of faith and worldview instruments have been developed (Fullerton and Hunsberger 1982; Hunsberger 1989; Hill and Hood 1999; Benson, Donahue, and Erickson 1993), most can be described as "too broad and lacking in depth or the opposite extreme of being so direct and even somewhat hyper-conservative in nature" (Taylor 2009, 127). In addition, many such instruments have been developed in non-Christian school settings, such as in Christian colleges and universities; while such instruments could theoretically be adapted to the K–12 setting, most lack the required robust field testing and refinement for such adaptation.

Spiritual Disciplines

Spiritual formation is naturally concerned with the cultivation of spiritual disciplines and habits consistent with a life of faith. According to Smith et al. (2021), no consideration of students' spiritual formation should neglect to consider spiritual practices (Willard 2002; Spears 2005; Harrison 2018).

One spiritual discipline commonly considered in research is church attendance. Descriptive research has found church attendance may support flourishing faith. Olwyn (2016) surveys families in Great Britain and finds the majority of Christians who attended church once a month or more frequently want their children to share their faith. Krause and Ellison (2007) find both church attendance and prayer life are significantly associated with commitment to faith in older adults. In their study of late adulthood, Wink and Dillon (2002) consider church attendance to be evidence of spiritual maturation.

Previous studies have considered the frequency of church attendance, but do not find consistent evidence of a significant relationship with measures of faith. Brickhill (2010) documents a significant relationship between frequency of church attendance and PEERS composite scores in Christian middle school students. Similarly, Chen, Hinton, and VanderWeele (2021) find some association between religious school attendance and increased frequency of religious service attendance when compared with public school counterparts. Alternatively, Rutledge (2013) failed to detect a correlation between adolescents' church attendance, Sunday school or youth service participation, or parental church attendance and PEERS composite scores. If a life of faith committed to consistent church attendance is indeed a marker of flourishing faith (Hebrews 10:25), it may be that frequency of church attendance is a poor proxy for commitment to a faith community, that the PEERS test does not measure sufficient variation in faith commitment, or both.

Well-Being

Biblically, wellness is viewed as wholeness and peace that is not circumstantial, but rather, covenantal, through faith, and providential, from God (Deuteronomy 12:28; Ephesians 6:3; Philippians 4:8–9). Research also uncovers evidence of associations between Christian education, or spiritual disciplines that may be found in Christian education, and wellness. A longitudinal outcome-wide analysis of various sectors found religious school attendance was associated with favorable health outcomes (Chen, Hinton, and VanderWeele 2021). One study found that religious involvement for Hungarian high school students was a protective factor against substance abuse, particularly for female students (Kovacs, Piko, and Fitzpatrick 2011). Another study of parents and adolescents found a positive association between religiosity and overall life satisfaction (Krok 2018). Gottfried and Kirksey (2018) found that students enrolled in Catholic elementary school demonstrated higher levels of self-discipline, were less likely to be disruptive, and exhibited more self-control than private or public school peers. Finally, a study specifically in a Christian school context found the spiritual discipline of Sabbath-keeping associated with psychosocial wellness (Cheng, Lee, and Djita 2022).

Political and Civic Outcomes

Christians serve as ambassadors for God's Kingdom, participating in secular frameworks honorably, while advancing the gospel through word and deed (Matthew 22:21; Romans 13:1–7; 1 Timothy 2:1–2). Christian school development of student civic-mindedness and participation outcomes should therefore reflect the head-heart-hands model and look differently than secular civic outcomes. Indeed, graduates of faith-based schools are more likely to engage in voluntarism as well as give to charitable organizations, including those other than churches (Wolf 2007; Casagrande, Pennings, and Sikkink 2019; Sikkink 2018b; Cheng and Sikkink 2020). Likewise, students' Christian school attendance is associated with a higher likelihood of becoming registered voters (Chen et al. 2021).

Academic Outcomes

Christians are called to pursue excellence (Philippians 4:8) and work heartily in all things (Colossians 3:23), doing all things to the glory of God (1 Corinthians 10:31). Evidence of flourishing faith may include excellence in academics as well. Research findings into Christian school academic outcomes vary. Lee and Price (2022) find consistent comparative ACSI members school academic performance in reading and mathematics to be over national norms. Pakaluk (2021) found that institution-to-student faith homogamy may also contribute positively to student learning gains relative to students in faith-mismatched schools. With respect to academic attainment, a Cardus report found that while graduates of Protestant Christian schools did not differ from their public-school peers, Protestant Christian private school postsecondary matriculation was found to be less competitive than that of Catholic and non-religious private schools (Pennings and Wiens 2011). This finding is consistent with research that shows Protestant school leaders prioritize other goals above college preparation (Sikkink 2012; Lee 2021; Lee, Cheng, and Wiens 2021).

Hospitality and Inclusion

Christian school development of student inclusivity and hospitality is operationalized in light of scripture through our identity as image bearers of God (Luke 19:1–10, Mark 3:1–6, John 5:1–29). Christ provides the pattern for replication through repeated demonstrations of reconciliation, inclusion, and hospitality. To this end, Anderson's (2003, 2011) research into *imago Dei* and reconciliation supports the idea of Christian school provision of inclusive special education instruction and biblical hospitality directed toward marginalized populations and students with disabilities. Similarly, Oosterhuis (2002) posits that the ideological aim of inclusivity among Christian schools within the Reformed tradition can be realized when this template is embraced by multiple stakeholders, including the family, church, school, and community. A study by Mercer (2015) of schools in thirty-five states found, on average, Christian schools demonstrate this inclusive pattern by proxy faithfully, with comparatively representative enrollment rates for children with disabilities as those of public schools.

Likewise, Catholic learning communities view special education provision and services as evidence of authentic understanding of their identity (Long and Schuttloffel 2006). Extending this reasoning, Rixford (1997) defined holistic worldview in part through intentional inclusion of students with disabilities in administrative and staff vision casting. ACSI's own research into flourishing schools found that responsiveness to special needs can be viewed as an area for opportunity within Christian schools. Qualitative research has found administrator implementation of special education programs to be challenging, yet academically and socially rewarding (Cookson and Smith 2011).

Family Outcomes

The work of telling the next generation applies not only to the Christian school, but also to Christian school students as well (Psalm 78:4). Joshua's legacy, for example, was that Israel served the Lord, not only all the days of Joshua, but "all the days of the elders who outlived Joshua and had known all the work that the Lord did for Israel" (Joshua 24:31). Thus, the family outcomes of Christian school graduates can be an important indicator of their flourishing faith. A growing body of research examines the family outcomes of Christian school graduates. Several studies find that graduates of Protestant schools are more likely to remain in an intact marriage than graduates of other sectors (Cheng et al. 2020; Wolf et al. 2022; Schwarz and Sikkink 2017). Sikkink (2018b) documents further evidence that attending a Christian college or university mediates the relationship between evangelical Protestant school attendance and marriage.

A Holistic Approach: Measuring Flourishing Faith

The broad scope of Christian education and the limitations of prior measures led ACSI to build upon its groundbreaking work with the Flourishing School Culture Instrument (FSCI) to develop the Flourishing Faith Index (FFI), a new survey instrument to measure how Christian schools can support their students' faith formation.

The development of the FFI was guided first and foremost by the Word of God. The instrument assumes faith formation to be a holistic process, though it can be broadly compartmentalized in the following dynamically developmental manner: head, heart, and hands (Garber 2007; Iselin and Meteyard 2010). However organized—whether head, heart, hands, "spirit, soul, and body" (1 Thessalonians 5:23), or "heart, soul, mind, and strength" (Mark 12:30)—faith formation is a comprehensive process that involves the whole person. Faith is formed at least in part in the mind. The Bible often describes faith as belief (e.g., Mark 1:15; John 20:31; 2 Thessalonians 2:13). As Alvin Plantinga writes, faith "isn't *merely* a cognitive activity, because it involves both the affections and the will. (It is a knowledge which is *sealed to our hearts* as well as to our minds.) But even if faith is *more* than cognitive, it is also and *at least* a cognitive activity" (2015, 58; emphasis his). Faith extends to the heart. Belief in Christ—believing in who He is and what He has done for us through His death on the cross and resurrection—is evidence of true heart change (Romans 10:9–10) and the product of divine heart surgery (Ezekiel 36:26–27). Faith is lived out in the hands. God also writes His law upon our hearts and causes us to walk according to His statutes (Jeremiah 31:31–34).

Of these pieces, the heart proves the most difficult to measure. External fruit can be observed and measured. Prior research has examined engagement in spiritual disciplines (including reading the Bible, prayer, and church attendance), commonly referenced as religiosity (e.g., Gunnoe and Moore 2002; Regnerus, Smith, and Smith 2004; Kimball et al. 2009; Petts 2011; Holder et al. 2016). More recent research on Christian schools has broadened outcomes to include acts of generosity, civic engagement, and vocational choice (Cheng, Djita, and Hunt 2022). But faith formation in the heart has thus far proven somewhat elusive to measure; some have commented that "the heart can't be measured" (Drexler and Bagby 2021, 1). Measures of the head or hands may serve as useful proxies of inclination or even attitudes toward religious activities, though they paint at best a partial picture of true faith formation without a measure of the heart.

After surveying the research literature, our research team drafted over two thousand survey items capturing faith in all three—the head, heart, and hands—and including measures of how school leadership, teaching and learning, relationships, and school institutional features are related to spiritual formation. Ultimately, we tested 764 items across seven constituent groups (teachers, administrators, support staff, board members, students, alumni, and parents) in a pilot study in the fall of 2022. The pilot study was completed by thirty-three schools, including twenty-nine U.S. schools broadly representing ACSI membership and four international schools. The pilot study will yield a statistical model of spiritual formation in Christian schools, as well as validated constructs that measure how Christian schools support spiritual formation. Thus, the FFI will enjoy several distinct advantages over prior instruments: 1) it is developed in a K–12 Christian school setting; 2) it is developed for practical application in K–12 Christian schools; and 3) it is developed to provide comprehensive feedback from all members of a school community. Our hope is that in the hands of school leaders, the FFI will be a powerful tool for understanding spiritual formation in a particular context and provide insights for how each school can best support flourishing faith.

We read in Hebrews that "faith is the assurance of things hoped for, the conviction of things not seen" (Hebrews 11:1). Faith is in some way connected to things that we can neither observe nor measure—things "hoped for" and "not seen." But as the evidence of such things, we can, however imperfectly, measure the growth of faith in our own lives as we are enabled both to die to sin and live to God (Romans 6:10). To truly live up to its name, a Christian education must be holistic in nature—training each child in head, heart, and hands. Training is inherently a spiritually formative process. Alongside families and churches, Christian schools play a critical role in forming minds, fostering attitudes, and cultivating disciplines that students may carry with them for their entire lives. Measurement is the first step to understanding how Christian schools can more faithfully—and perhaps more effectively—support the work of families and churches in nurturing faith in the next generation. To have truly flourishing schools, we must find evidence of flourishing faith that can in turn inform our practices in schools. By providing reliable measures, the Flourishing Faith Index can serve as a powerful tool for Christian schools to understand how they can most effectively support churches and families in nurturing faith in the coming generation.

Part 2:
Christian School Perspectives

The Leadership Perspective: Christian Education's Distinctives

Larry Taylor and Becki Rust

Prior to becoming ACSI's president in 2019, Dr. Larry Taylor served as the head of school at Prestonwood Christian Academy in Plano, Texas, for twenty years. Before that, he held leadership positions, including head of school, at The First Academy in Orlando, Florida, for twelve years. In this interview, ACSI Thought Leadership Project Coordinator, Becki Rust, asks Dr. Taylor about his perspective on spiritual formation and biblical worldview in the Christian school.

BR: Can you describe what the words *spiritual formation* and *biblical worldview* mean to you?

LT: Let me focus first on spiritual formation. I strongly believe that spiritual formation is the process of being conformed to the image of Jesus Christ for the glory of God and for the sake of others. The apostle Paul writes in 2 Corinthians 3:17–18, "Now the Lord is the Spirit, and where the Spirit of the Lord is, there is freedom. And we all, with unveiled face, beholding the glory of the Lord, are being transformed into the same image from one degree of glory to another. For this comes from the Lord who is the Spirit." Spiritual formation involves being conformed to the image of Christ. And I think that the focus of spiritual formation is the Holy Spirit, who is guiding this ongoing journey toward union with God. And I think the response from us to that process is submission. Spiritual formation is an organic, lifelong, holistic process. Our submission to that process enables the Holy Spirit to form right thinking in us, or orthodoxy, as well as the right behaviors, or orthopraxy. And that happens both with individuals and then with communities. So spiritual formation is the process of becoming like Jesus.

A biblical worldview is a cohesive set of beliefs, centered on God's Word as the absolute truth that tells the story of Creation, Fall, Redemption, and Glorification. There are many thinkers who have addressed worldview in depth and in a positive way. For me personally, although there were many prominent theologians before him that developed the concept of biblical worldview, I think Francis Schaeffer stimulated thinking around how Christians rooted their thought and actions in their foundational commitment to God's Word. He talked and wrote extensively about orthodoxy complemented by orthopraxy—the essential set of principles that one's values are shaped by a belief system grounded in God's Word, and which subsequently defined our actions. God's Word is the lens we look through when developing our views for every area of life. David Gushee and Glen Stassen (2016) in *Kingdom Ethics* then defined the worldview as a cohesive set of beliefs, through which people view the world and thus consciously set their life course. James Sire's (2020) book, *The Universe Next Door*, is also a seminal work in contemplating the fundamental questions that shape one's worldview.

One of the great contemporaries, David Naugle (2005), integrated the biblical concept of the heart into worldview—he argued that yes, worldview is a coherent set of beliefs, but biblically speaking, it is also a fundamental orientation of the heart. And so it's a fine line between spiritual formation and worldview. One could certainly argue that as we are conforming to the image of Christ, or being formed spiritually, we are also developing our worldview.

BR: What key scriptures would you highlight as being crucial to your understanding of spiritual formation and biblical worldview?

LT: There are several. I'd start with Romans 12:1–2, where the apostle Paul writes, "I appeal to you therefore, brothers, by the mercies of God, to present your bodies as a living sacrifice, holy and acceptable to God, which is your spiritual worship. Do not be conformed to this world, but be transformed by the renewal of your mind, that by testing you may discern what is the will of God, what is good and acceptable and perfect." This is a key scripture when we're talking about both spiritual formation and biblical worldview development. In addition, one scripture that we often view too simplistically is Luke 2:52, "And Jesus increased in wisdom and stature and in favor with God and man." I would argue that this verse points to some very important dimensions—wisdom, stature, favor with God, and favor with man—which speak to both formation and worldview for the believer.

Finally there's really a thread through all of the apostle Paul's writing, in terms of what encourages spiritual formation and worldview—as well as what can discourage, or even sabotage, both. We see this when Paul writes in Colossians 2:6–8, "Therefore, as you received Christ Jesus the Lord, so walk in him, rooted and built up in him and established in the faith, just as you were taught, abounding in thanksgiving. See to it that no one takes you captive by philosophy and empty deceit, according to human tradition, according to the elemental spirits of the world, and not according to Christ." That's a powerful passage when we're talking about spiritual formation and biblical worldview, because he points out that there are worldviews other than a biblical worldview—he mentions philosophy and human tradition. There are belief systems that can take one captive. So the implications are very deep for us, that there is a right way to think and to be formed, and there is clearly a wrong way. Christian schools have the opportunity to help shape and nurture students in the right direction.

BR: How would you say spiritual formation and biblical worldview development relate to the mission of the Christian school?

LT: I think it's the distinctive of a Christian school. If spiritual formation and biblical worldview development are not the priority of Christ-centered education, I would question whether that school is authentically Christian. Of course there are multiple influences on the development of a child's heart and mind, the most important being parents. But the Christian school assists the parents. And when considering that many of our Christian schools have parents who are not Christian, then by default, the school can actually be the primary influencer of a child's spiritual formation. We know that around the world Christian schools have a variety of admissions practices, whether they accept children from only Christian households or from families of any background, but the mission of the Christian school can be the same of spiritual formation and biblical worldview development.

BR: And what's the role of school leadership in prioritizing biblical worldview development and spiritual formation in their schools?

LT: I think the role of the leader is paramount. I often use the metaphor of a ship's rudder. School leaders, like the rudder, are really setting the direction for the school. So if the school is going to focus on these areas, that has to be the priority of the leaders, which includes the trustees of the school. And if the school is a ministry of a church, that includes pastors. The role of the leader is to adhere to an organizational discipline that it is presenting, promoting, practicing, and then preserving those practices that train teachers and students in these areas.

Practically speaking, regarding teachers, we know that when we hire Christian teachers that this doesn't necessarily mean they have a biblical worldview. There's not only a shortage of teachers, there's a shortage of Christian teachers who have a biblical worldview. So we need to assume that our staff will need ongoing training of their worldview, and in the process of integrating God's Word, into whatever they are teaching. We also need to make sure that the school has stated student aspirations related to graduates embracing a biblical Christian worldview—a portrait of a graduate. This is an ongoing process for Christian school educators—we must intentionally integrate biblical principles into all of the instructional and curriculum objectives. This includes the co-curriculum, because realistically, everything that a school does is curriculum. Every second that a Christian school teacher has with a student is an opportunity for spiritual formation and biblical worldview development. Without this perspective, it is easy to compartmentalize certain parts of the school. And the leader has to keep an eye on this, by holding that rudder steady in all areas of the school.

BR: What kinds of unique or particularly effective efforts did you and your teams develop in your schools to help students grow spiritually and in their biblical worldview?

LT: At Prestonwood Christian Academy, we started with a commitment that 100 percent of our faculty and even our staff would understand the fundamental foundations of a biblical worldview and Christ-centered spiritual formation. So we had six to eight certified trainers for our school, faculty and administrators who had been trained in a recognized process of biblical worldview integration into all the disciplines—science, history, math, English, all of them—not just Bible class. And so they were certified and they created a special training for new teachers that we hired, regardless of how many years they had been teaching previously. This training was thirteen hours long, divided into three or four sessions throughout the year, and was led by one of the certified trainers. This was a very specific program because it helped transmit our ethos, our culture, and to develop congruency among our teachers. We didn't just assume when we hired a teacher that they had already been trained, so our core program was to train teachers specifically in how to integrate God's Word into specific curriculum objectives and so forth.

We also had a Biblical Worldview Institute that was highly successful. It was held once a year for three days, and we had six categories that we would rotate through as the theme of the institute—for example, the business and corporate world, the political sphere, ministry, education, and so on. Students, faculty, and parents all attended. We would bring in speakers related to these themes, but I would say that 75 percent of the time, students were not just sitting there and listening. We wanted to model how within the Christian world, people can disagree with each other. So we had relevant topics that our students were experiencing, especially in high school, and we would have debates or panels that would discuss issues. But I think the secret sauce was what we did before and after the institute, which was small groups being led by faculty members. So even before the institute began, we had these small groups preparing our kids to think critically, and then afterward we used the small groups to get feedback from students on what they heard and what they learned. We wanted students to articulate their thoughts, and so we had to train our teachers on small group dynamics and how to cultivate an atmosphere and environment where students could be vulnerable and transparent. If a student had a doubt, we wanted those small groups to be safe. In order to develop a child's worldview, you have to see and hear from them. So these small groups gave us tremendous opportunity to see where our students were in their thinking.

Importantly, we measured the effectiveness of these programs. For example, during the re-enrollment process, we had a mandatory survey that had to be completed in order to re-enroll. And we had about ten or fifteen questions on the survey that were intentional to help us measure the effectiveness of various efforts in these areas. And the feedback allowed us to tweak the programs over the years as we ensured that they were not only effective but also always improving.

BR: What is the relationship between Christian schools and parents when it comes to the spiritual formation of their students, and how can Christian schools encourage parental engagement?

LT: I think the Christian school has the most unique opportunity when you think about other ministries, to work with parents specifically around the spiritual formation of their students. I'm not saying that the church is not doing their job or other parachurch ministries aren't doing their job. It's just the reality that schools have children from eight to twelve hours a day. And so we have that unique opportunity.

At the same time, I had a saying in our school: the spiritual health of a school is based on the health of the living room at home. Overwhelmingly, the research still says that parents are the number one influencer of a child maintaining their commitment to Christ for life. Barna's research found among Christian evangelical parents in the United States that 93 percent believed that they were the ones responsible, according to God's Word, for their child's spiritual development. That's the good news. The bad news was that 88 percent of those same parents did not feel confident to lead the spiritual development of their children.

At Prestonwood, we worked to come alongside parents to help equip them in that. Probably like many Christian schools, we partnered with churches to put on parenting and marriage conferences. But one of the unique things we did was a parent institute called "Becoming a Kingdom Family." We offered a class during the evenings, during lunchtime, during the weekends—whenever it would be convenient for parents to attend. It trained Christian parents to become more confident in leading their children's spiritual development. And importantly, for non-Christian parents, it became a place to present the Gospel. And really for all parents, the class helped to distinguish being a parent who, cares about their child to being a parent who is ultimately responsible, according to God's Word, to be the leader of the spiritual development of their children. I believe strongly that Christian schools should have an intentional program, whatever they call it, to really encourage the spiritual formation and the biblical worldview of not just the students and teachers, but also the parents. That's why I was saying earlier that our Biblical Worldview Institute was also for parents. I think we have that great opportunity in Christian schools to create space and time to foster parents' spiritual growth.

The last thing I'd say is that it's important for the head of school and key leaders in the school to be the ones leading these parent programs. This is an opportunity for a school leader to be with parents but in a totally different environment, and for parents to see a whole new side of that school leader. Parents could see me as a father and a husband, not just the head of school, and I'd use that opportunity to be very intentional in sharing where I'd failed as a parent or where I was on my spiritual journey. And as a result, parents get to see that no one's perfect. Most school leaders are only visible at back-to-school night or formal programs. So this parent ministry gives school leaders an opportunity to be transparent, to be vulnerable, and to build deep relationships with parents.

BR: What do you think are the biggest challenges facing Christian schools when it comes to forming students' biblical worldview and helping them to grow spiritually, and how can schools, leaders, and teachers overcome those challenges?

LT: I think the biggest challenge is that the primary influencers of a child's spiritual formation and biblical worldview formation are becoming more and more secular. And there's research that supports that, and certainly scripture does—we can go back to Colossians 2:6–8, where the apostle Paul warns us about empty and deceptive philosophies. Cultural Christianity can surface in many areas around the world—just because a parent says they are a Christian as they're going through the admissions process, doesn't necessarily mean that they're thinking Christianly. It's the same for our faculty and staff—if the end goal is to produce that portrait of a graduate that prioritizes spiritual formation and the biblical worldview, then our Christian teachers themselves need to have a mature biblical worldview and know how to teach from that perspective.

Overcoming those challenges begins with having the core leaders who have a strong conviction to never compromise on the commitment of spiritual formation and biblical worldview formation. If the conviction is there, leaders will find a way to train teachers and have special programs and ensure the curriculum is fully integrated biblically. This conviction also has to extend to trustees, who are responsible to hire the right CEO of their school and to evaluate the CEO, as well as provide and steward the resources for all of the above. It begins with the leaders being deliberate and intentional. Leaders should not be authoritarian of course. They should obviously be ambassadors for Christ in leading their schools to overcome these challenges. But it has to begin with the leaders.

BR: So, having been a school leader and now as president of ACSI, what encouragement would you offer to Christian school leaders and teachers when it comes to the spiritual formation and biblical worldview of their students, especially in today's day and age?

LT: My encouragement to Christian school leaders is really two things. First, God is bigger than anything that this world has to offer. I was talking to a friend recently who is an evangelist, and I asked him what his greatest challenge is—what he's seeing out there in the world. And he had an interesting response—he said "the spirit of cynicism." He explained that among adults, there seems to be a cynical, defeatist mentality—like this world is just getting too secular and too challenging. And so my encouragement to Christian school leaders and teachers is that regardless of how crazy the world gets, we know the end of the story. There is nothing in the culture that's bigger than our God, even if it is affecting students and families. The leader has an opportunity and a responsibility to create a culture of biblically based positive thinking, rooted in the truth that God has not given us a spirit of fear. We need to remember that there's nothing that God can't do.

I think the second thing I would say to encourage leaders and teachers is that we are in ministry, and as such we truly care about our students and school families. We have a strong sense of being called to this work. But the downside is that this can lead to becoming burned out. Not necessarily the physical toll of leading and teaching, but the emotional, the mental, the spiritual, and the overall well-being. So my encouragement for leaders and teachers is to make sure that their spiritual life, their heart, their soul—that they're healthy. I'm convinced that everyone needs a personal spiritual development plan and that families need a family plan, which I wrote about in my book *Running with the Horses*. And as part of that plan, to develop the discipline of checking weekly, monthly, and annually on how we're doing on our goals for the year—how are we growing spiritually, how is our physical activity, how are our relationships, and how is everything in our lives that contributes to well-being? Because if we are not intentional around our spiritual health, if we are not putting guardrails on our time, then we can easily become consumed by ministering to other people and become burned out. We have to be well in order to lead well.

So first, our God is bigger than anything in this culture, and second, take care of your heart. Proverbs 4:23 says to guard your heart, for out if it is the wellspring of life. And so leaders and teachers need to guard their hearts so that they can be healthy as they create schools that form students spiritually and help them to develop a biblical worldview.

The Teacher Perspective: Purposeful Cultivation
Mitch Evans

There is probably no more important categorical distinction that makes a Christian school "Christian" than the inclusion of spiritual formation and biblical worldview integration (BWI). The number of books, articles, dissertations, and blogs devoted to these related concepts is overwhelming. Yet, despite the abundance of material readily available, I would argue that a good number of teachers struggle with the "how" of spiritual formation and BWI. There is no questioning the "why"—we are called to be salt and light in our world and to do so, we need to understand how biblical principles affect the way we live and act.

So, what is it about the "how" that proves difficult, if not elusive, for many teachers? I would offer that part of the problem is that we treat biblical knowledge like we do other avenues of content, in that we have our Bible classes alongside our math classes. The confusion comes into play we when try to integrate calculus with the conquest of Canaan. How do these subjects interact? But taking this even further, we miss out on the application side of our understanding of the Bible. How do we know students understand academic concepts? We test and measure the *performance* of our students in that area. However, regarding spiritual matters, we fall short in this area when our assessment is limited to strict knowledge. In our ever-increasing attempts to quantify success in schools, we believe that doing well on a Bible test equates with spiritual formation or a good integration of biblical worldviews (Matthew 7 contains a story of how those who would probably do well on a Bible test still end up being told by Jesus, "I never knew you; depart from me."). Our students understand both the nuances of advanced biology as well as they can explain worldview issues, so we think that spiritual formation has taken place.

The difference that we miss is that the nuances of advanced biology are demonstrated in application—the student completes a lab, performs an experiment, or solves a problem. In other words, the student *does* something. In the Bible example, the student *states* something. So how do we truly know that the truths being taught are creating lasting change in our students? How can we approach spiritual formation and BWI in a way that would develop the types of graduates who would be able to impact their society for Christ? How can we "demystify" BWI so that authentic BWI is taking place in every classroom in our Christian schools?

We need a different philosophical approach as well as a different pedagogy. What follows is a way of viewing both education in general and students in particular that leads to an understanding of why a new pedagogical approach is needed—namely what I call a *pedagogy of cultivation*, that gets our students *doing* over and above *knowing* when it comes to spiritual formation and BWI.

A Philosophical Assumption

As a byproduct of the Enlightenment, education has been seen fundamentally as a rational venture (Hoffecker 2007). While there is not enough space to unpack the anthropological considerations, it suffices to say that the post-Enlightenment educational system functions as if humans are *thinking things* only (or at least primarily). Thus, learning is defined as the ability to retain and recite knowledge and is seen as the highest goal. Only recently has modern education seen a shift away from this model of thinking. For example, consider the original Bloom's taxonomy compared to the updated version. In the original, the highest level is *evaluation*. The updated version has *creating* at its peak, implying that the physical use of information should be the highest goal of teaching. Echoes of this type of approach are found in the popularity of project based learning and real world applications beyond mere recall (Anthony and Benson 2003). Teachers are beginning to realize that a more holistic view of the student is called for—one that understands we are beings who *do* beyond *think* and *know*. There is a *doing* that evidences full understanding of the content. As the chef says, "The proof is in the pudding."

How does an understanding of our students as *doers* rather than merely *thinkers* shape our view of BWI and spiritual formation? I believe it is found in the first five books of the Old Testament. Genesis 1 contains two fundamental truths to our understanding of humanity, namely our identity and our calling. Regarding our identity, Moses, through the inspiration of the Holy Spirit, records that humans (male and female) were created in the image of God. In ancient Near East culture, royals were considered to bear the image of their regional god (Pratt, Jr. 2022). Part of that designation implied that these rulers were to seek the will and wisdom of their god and apply it as they rule here on earth. For God to provide that label for us means we are to do the same: seek God's wisdom and will and then use our abilities to apply that wisdom in our daily lives.

But added to that image bearer designation is a call (Guinness 2003). Christians are called be fruitful, multiply, and have dominion over the earth. Too often, we minimize those verses to simple childbearing and creation care. The Creation Mandate includes them but goes well beyond (Wenham 2000). Simply put, Adam and Eve were tasked with taking the goodness of God's creation and spreading it out over a wilderness. They were to go out and multiply the goodness, fullness, and completeness of the Garden. In short, they were called to cultivate God's version of a flourishing life both in and beyond themselves.

Fast forward a few books to Deuteronomy. In chapter 6, Moses provided the pathway to this flourishing. He exhorts Israel to heed to his words so that they may multiply greatly (v. 3) and the summary of his words is in verses 4–5. Because God is who He is, we are called to love Him with the whole of our being. What follows are the commands of God. The implication is clear: to love God is to obey God; to obey God is to *do* what God commands. Moses' words are just as applicable in the classroom—we are to teach the words of God but also instruct in how to do the words of God, namely, how to live a flourishing life and bring about God's rule and reign in this age.

Having briefly established the concept that humans are *doers* beyond *thinkers*, and that we have a set identity (image bearers) and call (cultivators), we can now turn to the *how* of effective BWI in the classroom.

A Pedagogy of Cultivation

In the introductory essay to *Teaching and Christian Practice: Reshaping Faith & Learning*, Smith and Smith (2011) discuss how current Christian educational approaches tend to follow secular trends with an added spiritual stamp. There is chapel time. There is prayer. There is the presentation of the gospel. There are mission opportunities. But the essay argues (and I generally agree) that the actual pedagogy presented is more secular than Christian, and that the academic aspects consummate in the *doing* while matters of a spiritual nature stop at the *learning*.

The danger is that we run the risk of confusing "believing in God with believing ideas about God" (Neder 2019, 39). Neder argued that true belief in God will manifest itself in a life lived *before* God and *for* God. A life of obedience consists of being "at peace with him [God], with our neighbors, and with ourselves" (Neder 2019, 25). scripture is full of similar calls by Jesus and His apostles: "Follow me" (Matthew 4:19), "Go, and do likewise" (Luke 10:37), "Feed my lambs" (John 21:15), "Whatever you do, do all to the glory of God" (1 Corinthians 10:31), and "Be doers of the word" (James 1:22). The connection is clear: proper knowledge culminates in proper action.

The Gospel of Matthew contains one of the best examples of this process of how teachers can move their students from mere knowledge to action. After establishing the *bone fides* authority of Christ, Matthew, in chapters 5–10, presents a master Teacher at work, instructing His disciples in both the knowledge and application of the scriptures. The Sermon on the Mount (chapters 5–7) serve as the didactic portion of instruction, with Jesus explaining how a life that honors God is to be lived. In chapters 8 and 9, Matthew shifts to describe what Jesus does. A brief survey of the sections summarizes these events: healing, casting out of demons, calming, calling, and teaching. Chapter 9 concludes with the following:

> And Jesus went throughout all the cities and villages, teaching in their synagogues and proclaiming the gospel of the kingdom and healing every disease and every affliction. When he saw the crowds, he had compassion for them, because they were harassed

and helpless, like sheep without a shepherd. The He said to His disciples, "The harvest is plentiful, but the workers are few. Therefore, plead with the Lord of the harvest to send out workers into His harvest." (Matthew 9:35–39, NASB)

Chapter 10 contains the crux of application for a pedagogy of cultivation. Jesus did not provide a written test or assign an essay about what He taught them. Instead, He sent them out to do likewise. The apostles were given authority to do the very things Jesus did: heal the sick, cleanse lepers, cast out demons, give freely, and comfort others. What Jesus expected of them was to go and *do* what He both taught and modeled. That is the mindset that is missing in many classrooms that struggle with BWI and spiritual formation. The model is presented clearly in the Bible—go and do likewise. In short, Jesus taught His disciples (and us) to be true image bearers and engage with a broken world in a way that the flourishing life of the kingdom of God is put on full display. So how can this engagement, this culture fixing and building, be seen in our classrooms?

As teachers, we need to capture the imaginations of our students about what a gospel-lived life can look like (Prior 2018). In *Christian Apologetics*, C.S. Lewis wrote: "What we want is not more little books about Christianity, but more little books by Christians on other subjects—with their Christianity latent" (1970, 91). In other words, what we need are Christians engaging in their myriad of disciplines in a way that is uniquely Christian. In my own classroom, I tell stories of how through God's grace, medical research has reduced disease (cure), bioengineers are designing prosthetics to enable amputees to increase function (care), bioethicists are working to protect the dignity of humanity (confront), and farmers are developing methods for growing food for impoverished areas (cultivate). There are countless examples of areas where Christians can engage in their communities (Stonestreet and Kunkle 2017); those examples need to be presented (and practiced when possible) in our classrooms. Teachers also can provide students with opportunities to take what they are learning about the Bible to its practical applications but in ways that are specifically geared toward the academic content at hand. [See chapters 7 and 9 of this monograph for examples of ways to accomplish this in Christian schools.]

Four Components of a Cultivating Classroom

With a framework in place for what authentic BWI looks like in a Christian school classroom, we can now turn to what I consider four components of classrooms that would have authentic BWI. In other words, if these components are present, intentional, and observable, then there is a high likelihood of authentic BWI also taking place.

Corem Deo

My mentor often tells the story of a time when he was a principal going through formal planned observations with his staff. There was one teacher who seemed to knock the observation out of the park, earning high marks in every category. As my mentor started to leave the classroom, one of the students leaned back in his chair and quietly asked, "Did you enjoy the show?" The student's message was clear: this was not a normal classroom experience for students. Why did this teacher behave in a different manner than before? Simply because the teacher knew the teacher was being observed.

While this story has obvious implications for consistency in teaching, it has broader implications because we are constantly being observed by God. *Corem Deo* is a theological term meaning "living before the face of God." Just as we should teach as if our principal is in the room, we should also teach as if God is in the room ... simply because He is (Psalm 139:7–12).

The key idea of this component is that we live every aspect of our lives before the face of God; thus, every aspect of our schools and classrooms should have a higher end in mind. Moving from the lesser to the greater, if the chief end of humanity is to glorify God and enjoy Him forever (The Westminster Shorter Catechism 2020), then the chief end of a Christian school should be the same. If humans fulfill this chief end by the dedication of the whole of their lives to God, then schools should be no different. Christian schools will find their ultimate fulfillment when every school element is designed and acted upon to (a) glorify God and (b) live a life that enjoys His gifts and blessings in a proper manner.

A couple of ways of accomplishing this chief end is by consciously operating in the presence of God and under the authority of God. Take classroom management for example. While there are many different standards among classrooms across the world, if my method of classroom management does not point my students to the presence and authority of God, it is a meaningless set of procedures. Likewise, if my curriculum does not point my students to the presence and authority of God, it is meaningless.

All the components of a school have their own purposes. Yes, we want our students to behave a certain way, we want our athletic teams to be successful, we want our students to excel academically, and we want our fine arts programs to perform at a high level. But these are all secondary compared to Paul's words in Colossians that whatever we do in word and deed, we do in the name of Christ (Colossians 3:17). The authority Christ gives His disciples and now us, empowered by the Holy Spirit, is not so that we can increase our enrollment or make a name for our school; it is given so that His Kingdom may grow, and His name be magnified.

In short, simply because we operate under the presence and authority of God, there is not, to paraphrase Abraham Kuyper, one square inch of a Christian school that God does not claim as His for His use and purposes. When we understand that all aspects of our schools serve that goal, then we can see how the whole of the school, from operations to *Oklahoma!*, from classrooms to carline, from finances to football games, serves as an avenue for the spiritual formation of our stakeholders.

Consistency

A second component that should be considered when evaluating the effectiveness of BWI for a classroom is *consistency*. Most schools have some sort of expected student outcomes or portrait of a graduate where they list out the qualities that should be present in students as they walk across the stage in their caps and gowns. It should be the priority of the school, then, that every grade works with the end goal of those outcomes. Thus, all staff should have a common goal in mind in their work so there can be a consistent approach from class to class and grade to grade. Much like our work is to be done mindful of the presence and authority of God, our work should also be done in a future-oriented manner. While this is obvious in an educational setting in that basic addition will come before PEMDAS which then allows for advanced math, it should be similar in our spiritual formation plan.

It is not difficult to identify the hot cultural topics of our day. It is also not difficult to understand that some topics are too complex or age-inappropriate for some of our students (Stonestreet and Kunkle 2017). However, complex topics always have simple foundations. The method by which we handle this is no different than how we handle integral calculus: start with the foundations early and then build on them throughout the years. Take human trafficking for example. It would not be right or wise to expose kindergarteners to the world of the *Taken* films, but it would be right and wise to introduce them to the concept of being created in the image of God and how that provides intrinsic worth and value to all humans. As they age, they can be taught about how the effects of sin cause people to mistreat others because they value them less. In higher grades, students can learn and discuss slavery and human trafficking as a reality, culminating in discussions on the Christian response to this issue.

Just as the math department plans out a scope and sequence of development in math skills, schools should plan out a scope and sequence of what would lead to a flourishing spiritual formation in their students. What are the issues we believe our students need to be able to address and respond to in a biblical manner and what are the incremental steps we must take to get them to that point? What subjects are best equipped to teach and model those steps? It will take the focused work of the whole school to accomplish this rather than segmented Bible lessons here and there, hoping that the senior apologetics class can tie everything together. There must be a purposeful, consistent approach to the teaching and training of our students in spiritual issues, and this approach should be woven into every aspect of our Christian schools.

Un-Comfortable

Every night at 9PM, my gym posts the scheduled workout for the next day. With few exceptions, there is a high probability that workout will consist of some movement or exercise that either I am not good at or just simply despise (looking at you, thrusters). The temptation is high either to skip or modify the workout to make it something more in my comfort zone. I have learned, however, those exercises I don't like are exposing weakness and deficiencies in my overall fitness. And those are the areas that need my attention the most. Embracing the uncomfortable makes me a better athlete.

The same holds true in spiritual formation. A teacher dedicated to authentic BWI must discuss all topics that are relevant to living a flourishing life in this cultural moment, not just the ones that are pleasant or easy. My parents often lament what the future holds for their grandchildren. In our discussions, we almost always come back to the point that (a) God is sovereign over all human history and (b) in His perfect wisdom, He has seen it fit to ordain our lives to exist in this moment in history. In short, we are to work the soil we are assigned to bring about spiritual fruit in our lives and in the lives of others (Crouch 2008). The difficulties of our current culture are no surprise to God and His call remains unchanged: teach and make disciples. Thus, we are called to engage in this culture, in all its brokenness and sorrow as well as all its hope and potential for redemption. We cannot avoid the topics or issues that we do not feel equipped to discuss or simply make us feel uncomfortable. We must be willing to tackle these issues and redeem them in a manner that advances the kingdom of God.

Just as we discussed earlier about age-appropriateness in teaching our children, we hear similar arguments regarding the presentation (or lack thereof) of biblical approaches to controversial topics: "Well, we do not want to put ideas into our students' heads" or "We do not want to expose them to certain ideas." Trust me—students already have ideas; they need to find biblically based answers! Difficult topics allow the beauty of a pedagogy of cultivation to flourish. Every *uncomfortable* topic provides a chance to turn to the *comfort* of the cross (Brooks 2014).

There is not one issue on the cultural docket that is not addressed by the four-act presentation of the metanarrative of the Bible. First, Creation provides the initial design of God. Second, the Fall explains how there is brokenness in our world due to the curse of sin. Third, Redemption speaks how Christ incarnate has come to break the effects of that curse so that we may live apart from its ultimate rule over our lives. Finally, the Bible promises a future Glorification in which we will experience life in abundance, free from the effects of sin and in ultimate flourishing. Since the Bible speaks to all issues in some fundamental, foundational manner, we should not shy away from its use in informing how our various content areas provide a picture of a flourishing life.

Just as Mordecai asked Esther to consider whether she was placed in the position she was in for such a time as this (Esther 4:14) and just as the men of Issachar understood the times during the reign of David and knew what Israel should do (1 Chronicles 12:32), we should consider a similar approach in the spiritual formation of our students. They have been placed in this particular moment in cultural history so that God can work through them to advance His Kingdom. If our students have been sovereignly ordained to live in this cultural moment, then we, as teachers, have also been sovereignly ordained to guide them into understanding and living a biblical life that models flourishing in the midst of current culture. We dare not do this on our own strength, but through the power and guidance of the Holy Spirit.

Culture

As stated earlier, authentic spiritual formation and BWI should be a hallmark of Christian schools. As such, spiritual formation and BWI should be an intentional component of a Christian school and built into all aspects of school life, especially the classroom. I would argue that the overall goal here is to make this process natural and seamless rather than awkward and forced. The earlier writings of James K. A. Smith are helpful here. The basic crux of his argument is that our actions and habits are formed by our desires and loves (J. K. Smith 2016; see Smith's triology of *Desiring the Kingdom, Imagining the Kingdom,* and *Awaiting the King*). Thus, we do (or we are) what we love. These ideas are not new. Augustine provides a similar argument. He writes, "In this life there are two loves in conflict in every temptation: the love of this world and the love of God. Whichever one wins out draws the lover like gravity in its direction. It is not through feet or wings but by desire that we come to God" (1995, 49). Or Jesus says: "For where your treasure is, there your heart will be also" (Matthew 6:21).

But seeking after the things of Christ is not the natural inclination of our hearts. Think about getting ready today. In putting on a shirt or pants or a pair of socks, you probably put in the same foot or same arm first every time you do so, yet you do so without even thinking about it. Years of getting dressed has established an automatic routine that comes naturally to us; it becomes a defining feature of who we are. Same with eating—we do not choose a salad over a slice of cake, for the simple reason that we love cake more than salad. Once our habits and desires are changed, our actions will follow. Smith translates this concept to learning, specifically learning that leads to spiritual formation (2016). The pedagogy in a Christian classroom should be created and organized to develop the habits of a life lived before God. We do not need more information that a salad is healthier than a cake; what we need is a change in our habits which inform our desires, so that we naturally choose the salad over the cake.

Thus, we need to create a culture where our students learn, watch, and participate in actions that will help develop a natural desire to love God and love others, through the help and enabling of the Holy Spirt. We need to teach our classes in such a way that our content helps them see how they can engage in culture in a meaningful way. The more they see this modeled in a developmental manner (i.e., age- and content-specific) and the more they practice applying learned biblical knowledge, the more natural a life lived in the presence of God becomes. BWI then becomes a natural outflow of a practiced life, both in and out of the classroom. Just as our students naturally put shoes on in a specific order day after day, they can naturally respond to a situation in a way that is loving toward God and others. While not formulaic, and the outcome we desire is not guaranteed (as proper teaching does not always equate to effective outcomes), we can create an educational environment where the goal is for BWI to become ingrained in who they are and how they act. In short, it can become their culture. But that only happens through *doing* spiritual matters repeatedly. Just as Jesus taught and led His disciples, we need to have our students move from *knowing* to *doing*.

A New Creation

So, what should spiritual formation and BWI look like in the classroom? It should consist of purposeful activities that teach students the truths of God's Word as it connects to a content area, which then engage those students in applying God's Word. This is done in the hope that the Holy Spirit will use those ingrained aspects of knowledge and habits to get students to love those around them as Christ loves them. In short, it is purposeful training to teach and model how to love the Lord their God with all of their heart, soul, strength, and mind, and love their neighbor as themselves.

One of my favorite songs is *Behold* by Propaganda, Sara Groves, and Audrey Assad (2019). In the first verse, Propaganda provides a contrast on the two ways humans are accomplices to this moment in history. At first, playing off the parable of the Good Samaritan, he speaks of how we tend to put ourselves in the place of all the characters, but in doing so we miss the main question: why is there madness on the road to Damascus? In short, we are accomplices because we are more like the robbers than we want to admit, participating in a culture of brokenness. But in the second part, he states that we are accomplices in God's redemptive plan for humanity. We are broken vessels, but broken vessels used by God to accomplish His will. The verse ends with a powerful couplet: "And when tomorrow came calling … he did a new thing with you and me. Hey, and when tomorrow came calling, he did a new thing, and he did it with you and me."

God, in His individual redemption, makes us a new creation (2 Corinthians 5:17), but then He uses His new creation to do something even greater—namely the redemption of the whole of creation. Our students need to capture a vision of *how* that is accomplished and how our vocations—be it teaching, medicine, law, caregiving, custodial, and all callings in between—can be used by God for His glory (Guinness 2003). In the full spectrum of a K–12 Christian education, a student should see how all areas of knowledge can and should be used to cure what is diseased, confront what is evil, care for what is broken, and cultivate what is good. It takes a general knowledge of all subjects but also of how they help us participate in God's redemptive plan for humanity. It is to that end that we as Christian educators pray and work, to the glory of God.

The Curricular Perspective: Biblical Worldview Integration
Debbie MacCullough

In the early 1990s, the Association of Supervision and Curriculum Development (ASCD) commissioned a group of educators to consider how coherency could take place in the public school curriculum in the United States. ASCD had recognized that students did not see learning as a unified whole and this led to a lack of clarity about learning and schooling. The research examined how American education might bring about a curricular unity, the results of which were compiled in a yearbook, *Toward a Coherent Curriculum* (1995). The editor, James A. Beane, stated, "A 'coherent' curriculum is one that holds together, that makes sense as a whole; and its parts, whatever they are, are unified and connected by that sense of the whole" (5).

The contributors wrote much about this coherent curriculum but were unable to define what the "whole" might be. Contributors suggested that an "integrated curriculum" must have an integrating core around which all of learning is connected. This suggestion led to a new focus on curriculum integration. Some of these integrating cores included problem solving, critical thinking, social justice, the arts, math and science, and many others, some of which became the focus of charter schools. However, the conclusion of the ASCD yearbook was disappointing in that the editor doubted if it was possible in a pluralistic society to decide on an "integrating core" that formed the knowledge most worth knowing and provided the "glue" for students to connect and appreciate all of learning.

As followers of Christ who desire to see the students in our Christian school flourish, I suggest that we have a superior overarching integrating core: a biblical worldview. This worldview will help us to solve problems, think critically, be aware of our role in justice, appreciate the arts, and so forth. By using a biblical worldview as our integrating core, our students can see the unity that God has designed in all they are learning.

The Integrating Core Model

The integrating core approach led to a movement in education where the use of "essential questions" as objectives became the trend (McTighe and Wiggins 2013). A teacher would write the learning objective and essential question for the students to see, allowing the students to understand the end goal (the "whole"). Next, the teacher would teach the "parts" of this whole, while promoting internalization and connections for students. This describes the typical teaching that has taken place for years across many school sectors.

When I was training undergraduate and graduate students in education, I would teach this integrating core model using a lesson model with elements. These elements have a long history of development in education, including the "Hook, Book, Look, Took" model from Larry Richards (Richards and Bredfeldt 1998, 2020); while they can be called different things, the specific terms used are not as important as the concepts underlying them. After describing the objective(s) and essential question(s), each lesson should start with an activity that cues any prior knowledge or experience that students might have relevant to what is to be learned. I called this part of the lesson "activation," but other words used might be "hook," "motivation," "opening activity," or "engage." Next, building on this activity, a second element is that of "new information" or "book." This is a time for students to take in—through reading, watching, or exploring—new or additional information that will help them to learn, answer the essential questions, and work toward the lesson objective. The next element is what I called "student processing" and involves activities for the students to do to make sense of what they have just learned. Students answer questions, connect the added information in new situations, organize the information into categories, or practice using a rule or principle. Finally, the last element is assessment, in which students' knowledge and achievement of learning objectives is measured.

It is important to note that there is often an iterative nature to a lesson. While there is an order that must take place, there is also the ability and often the need to go "back and forth" among the elements. For example, one lesson might be activation, new information, student processing, assessment—followed by more new information, student processing, additional activation for new information, and student processing, and then additional assessment.

Integrating Biblical Worldview

This model and cycle can be harnessed to create a coherent curriculum around the core of a biblical worldview. Teachers begin by developing and stating a worldview essential question related to the content of the lesson. Some examples of worldview questions are provided in Table 1 below, and are differentiated by school level. In order for the essential worldview question to be used effectively in planning, it must also have a biblical answer articulated beforehand, created either by or for the teacher.

Table 1. Sample Worldview Questions by School Level

Worldview Questions: Upper School Grades (adapted from Sire 2020)	Worldview Questions: Lower School Grades (adapted from MacCullough 2016)
1. What is prime reality—the ultimate or foundational reality?	1. What is real?
2. What is the nature of external reality/ the world around us?	2. Where did the world come from?
3. What is a human being?	3. Who am I?
4. What happens to a person at death?	4. What happens when I die?
5. Why is it possible to know anything at all?	5. How do we learn stuff?
6. Why is it possible to know what is right and wrong?	6. What's right and wrong?
7. What is the meaning of human history?	7. Why do we learn about the history past?
8. What life commitments are consistent with these beliefs?	8. How should I live because of what I believe?

A unit or lesson will highlight this question in the student processing activities. It will also allow the students to wrestle with how differing worldviews might answer the question and/or how the biblical worldview answers the question. This questions-based approach simplifies for teachers what to do to incorporate biblical worldview within their subjects. Questions such as, is there a God, what is a human being, how do we know right or wrong, is there life after death, what is the meaning of history, of external reality and the world around us, and so on are addressed throughout the regular curriculum, and not just limited to Bible classes (MacCullough 2016).

In creating units and lessons in this way, students are exposed to thinking biblically about all of life and learning, and one of the major results is a sense of unity. Students are enriched as they connect their lessons to a biblical worldview and distinguish beliefs that do not fit with a biblical view. This is a form of critical thinking. Using the biblical worldview as the integrating core provides opportunities for students to experience the value of all they are learning. The curriculum's coherency is overt and allows students to develop an integrated understanding of what they are learning, situated within a developing worldview.

What is being integrated? It is the student's mind that becomes integrated. As they explore how God's Word answers the major question of the lesson or unit, students measure, evaluate, and appreciate God's truth about His created order and about Himself. At the same time, students learn and retain information that does not cohere with God's perspective. Thus, in each subject, students grow in biblical worldview as their minds are transformed to God's Word rather than conformed to the pattern of the world, as the apostle Paul writes in Romans 12:2. [See the end of this chapter for a Biblical Worldview Integration Rubric, that can be used by classroom teachers and curriculum directors alike, to gauge the level of biblical worldview integration in a given course.]

Biblical Worldview Integration: An Example from Mathematics

I recall my days as a Christian school student in the 1970s and 1980s. I remember several times seeing an administrator enter our mathematics class. I knew this meant our teacher was being observed. Once I had experienced this a few times, I began to think to myself, "Here comes the 'God is a God of order' lesson" and usually, I was right. I am not denying that God is a God of order, nor that mathematics can show this to us well. I have been a mathematics teacher for years and see the glory of God's order in much that I have taught. What I am suggesting is that there was a singular focus on this one aspect (that God is a God of order) of how mathematics could help me better understand a biblical view of the world. Unfortunately, very few mathematics teachers (myself included in my early years) can tell you how our biblical worldview impacts our understanding of mathematics. When the administrator walks through the door to conduct observations is not the right time to figure this out. It takes time and forethought if we are to frame our lessons up front with a biblical lens.

One of the greatest challenges I have seen as I train teachers in writing lessons to help students to develop a biblical worldview is finding the right question or questions to ask. Often this struggle comes from teachers not knowing how to identify worldview questions addressed in their materials and therefore what the biblical answers might be to help the students discover. Christian Schools Australia (Benson et al. 2017) has created a powerful tool to use for thinking through the biblical worldview related to a particular concept. They used the Creation-Fall-Redemption-Restoration (CFRR) framework to guide teachers in thinking through a biblical worldview of a particular topic. With each part of the framework, they ask the teacher key questions.

I provide here an elementary unit I designed, related to division of fractions, to illustrate how this tool can be used to guide teachers to develop the worldview questions addressed in a topic. As a trained teacher of mathematics, I wanted to see if there was a way to help my students to intentionally develop a biblical view of the fractions they were learning about. This approach would allow my students to see and appreciate mathematics from God's perspective.

The first step was to analyze a broad biblical worldview related to the operations of multiplying and dividing fractions. Using the CFRR framework, I asked myself, "What was God's intention, at Creation, for fractions and operations on fractions?" Here is a list of some ideas along with the worldview question(s) they answer:

- God created humans to communicate quantitatively (answers the question, "What is a human being?" A human being can think quantitatively and spatially and can use that learning).
- God intended for us to be able to describe and use His creation quantitatively, and thus created us with the ability to model creation with symbols (also answers the question, "What is a human being?" Human beings can describe God's creation using the faculties with which God created us).
- Mathematics is logical and reasonable because of the nature of God, who is the Creator of mathematics (answers the question, "What kind of God is our God?" He is logical and reasonable and has given humans the capacity to think and reason about His creation).

Next, I thought about the Fall of mankind. What went wrong and how has God's purpose been distorted because of the Fall? I listed the following ideas (which continue to answer the big worldview questions):

- Human beings are fallen creatures and therefore do not reason or think perfectly.
- Our communication is flawed because of this fallen nature.
- Sometimes we find something difficult, and we lack perseverance because we are limited and fallen creatures.
- What we discover and think may not always be correct, including our mathematical models.

The third step was to consider our redemption. How does God want us to respond and care, as it relates to mathematical thinking? I thought of the following:

- We should work to be clear in our communication; it is God-honoring.
- We can work to understand God's creation in a quantitative way.
- We need to ask God to help us persevere when we struggle through something difficult.

The last step was to consider future restoration. Where is future hope found and what would restoration look like? Again, I listed some ideas:

- Fractions will not be scary because we will understand how they communicate and describe God's creation.

- We will persevere without frustration.
- Our brains will function as God intended and we will use fractions as part of the mandate to "subdue" (meaning use but not abuse) God's creation.

This activity of "brainstorming" regarding a biblical view of the concept of fractions and division of fractions allowed me to see, in writing, how to think biblically about mathematics such as fractions. I illustrate it here to demonstrate how a teacher, or group of teachers, can think through their content using the CFRR biblical worldview framework.

Although mentioned briefly in the initial bulleted list in this section, it is worth highlighting that I chose to focus on primarily on one worldview question throughout the entire unit: "What is the nature of human beings?" Because of the content of the unit, I focused on the biblical answer that human beings are created in the image of God and have the capacity to think quantitatively. We can model reality using quantities and physical models because God created us with this ability. God created both the knower (students) and the known (content) and therefore we can expect that God will help us understand His created principles, although we are limited by our humanity. Related to this question, my lesson also examined the purpose of human beings. Again, the content itself provided one biblical answer to this question: we are to use our abilities to glorify God. When we are dividing fractions and using the abilities God has given us, we can and should do this for His glory.

This brainstorming, or "lensing" as the workgroup from Christian Schools Australia has called the activity, helps the teacher to better visualize biblical worldview thinking as it is related to a particular concept. From this activity, the curriculum map can be created. Just as we map out the development of understanding a concept (such as division of fractions) over a few years of teaching, the worldview development can also be mapped out over a few years. An introductory unit on fractions could focus on how God has created us to communicate quantitatively. A more developed unit could focus on ways in which we can use this communication for God's glory. Within that mapping, teachers can provide activities and questions that will allow the students to critically analyze biblical worldview thinking about the content being learned.

Integrating the Core: The Curriculum Director's Role

When a school commits to helping students to develop a biblical worldview and states that the school's curriculum is taught from a "distinctly" Christian point of view, it is critical that the curriculum is well-planned to help the student intentionally develop this distinctive worldview in all areas of learning. The reality is that teachers need not only training for biblical worldview integration (discussed in the following chapter on faculty development), but also ongoing support. When a teacher is left to autonomously decide what worldview question is to be answered in a unit, often the same question (and sometimes the only question) is answered year after year.

Whether a full- or part-time position, one role of a curriculum director is to help teachers develop the school's overall curriculum with the appropriate worldview questions—and sequencing of those questions—throughout the curriculum. Another role is to work with teachers to explore the worldview questions and sub-questions related to their content area. This means that curriculum mapping should be done carefully, examining how content can help students, at each specific age, to develop their growing worldview in such a way that it becomes more in line with God's Word. The questions-and-answer approach to biblical worldview development allows for a well-designed curriculum to be laid out as different questions can be asked and answered according to those observed in the curriculum and resource materials.

Schoolwide curriculum mapping or curriculum planning has been around for over two decades and is essential to this process. Heidi Hayes-Jacobs (1997, 2004) has written much on curriculum mapping and how to use it effectively. Technology exists to assist school leaders and teachers in developing curriculum maps, and is easily adaptable to a worldview/essential questions approach. Unit objectives can include a required worldview question to be answered by students. Additionally, teachers can either be provided with or be asked to find the biblical answer to that question before teaching the unit. In the activities listed for the regular lessons, worldview processing activities can be included. Finally, when assessments are created, these should also include an evaluation of the student's biblical worldview understanding related to the unit question. This, in part, prevents teachers from simply tacking on a devotional or a verse that is not connected to the learning at hand.

Pulling all these approaches together will require curriculum directors to coordinate multiple aspects of curriculum development at their schools. Each school typically has a curricular review process and cycle, and all elements of biblical worldview integration planning can be included in this cycle (such as development and review of worldview questions, sequencing of those questions, approaches for integrating them into specific lessons, planning for assessment that includes worldview development, and recording and tracking all the above through the school's curriculum mapping system or process). Additionally, expected student outcomes (ESOs) should be correlated to the curriculum map. Lastly, the curriculum should be aligned with the school's mission, vision, philosophy of education, and clear definition of biblical worldview.

Continuing to build upon the prior example from mathematics and the teaching of operations with fractions, when the time to review mathematics arises in the school's curricular review cycle, the curriculum director can do the following to prepare mathematics teachers for the review. First, provide a training on what biblical worldview is, using the school's definition, and help the mathematics teachers understand how helping students develop a biblical worldview regarding mathematics will support the school's mission, vision, philosophy of education, and expected student outcomes. By preparing teachers to understand the purpose of their work and how it fits the school's overall aims, the curriculum director can properly orient teachers and better guide the work to be done in the review.

Next, those who will be working on the curriculum map should be prepared for how the school's mapping is done (software or paper, what should be included, how to connect to ESOs, etc.). Finally, teams of teachers can work on developing the mapping together. I suggest that the team first work to ask and answer the worldview questions in a manner similar to the example given prior in the chapter. After this, the team can work to decide at what grade level particular questions should be answered. Additionally, they can work on linking instructional strategies and assessments. Table 2 below provides a sample of what this might look like for the operations on fractions unit.

Table 2. Operations on Fractions

Big Idea, Worldview Questions, and Objectives	Standards and Schoolwide Expected Student Outcomes (ESOs)
Big Ideas: • Operations do not change regardless of the set of numbers. • We can model reality using fractions. **Worldview Question & Answer:** "What is the nature of humans?" Human beings are created in the image of God and have the capacity to think quantitatively. We can model reality using quantities and physical models because God created us with this ability. **Objectives (the student will be able to):** • Multiply and divide fractions. • Relate operations on fractions to those on whole numbers. • Model both multiplication and division of fractions. • Appreciate God's gift to model reality using fractions. • Explore ways to use fractions for God's glory.	**NCTM Process Standards:** Reasoning and Proof, Representation, and Communication. **NCTM Grades 6–8 Expectations:** Understand the meaning and effects of arithmetic operations with fractions, decimals, and integers. **Schoolwide ESOs:** • Develop a biblical worldview that permeates understanding of every subject. • Create new ways of thinking by exercising problem solving and collaboration skills. • Communicate well both in writing and orally.

Strategies/Best Practices Used for Instruction	Assessments
1. Modeling of fractions using rectangular model.	1. Model drawing of division of fractions.
2. Using understandings of fractions and division, create an algorithm for dividing fractions (word problem worksheet).	2. Write a division of fractions word problem.
3. Articulate created algorithm, use it, relate this to standard algorithm.	3. Use created algorithm to practice division of fractions.
4. Model multiplication of fractions using rectangular model.	4. Relate created algorithm to the standard algorithm.
5. Create word problems for both multiplication and division of fractions.	5. Model multiplication of fractions.
6. Explore how God created us with the ability to model reality mathematically. Discuss accuracy of fractions.	6. Write a multiplication of fractions word problem.
	7. Write a response to "how might we use modeling with fractions for God's glory?"

In addition to the unit map, a template for lesson plans should be developed and used by teachers to drill down on the specifics for each unit. This template should reflect the elements of the integrating core model discussed at the beginning of this chapter: 1) Lesson Objectives, 2) Essential Worldview Questions, 3) Activation Methods, 4) Concept/ Skill Development, 5) Student Processing Activities, and 6) Assessment. Finally, once the mapping is completed by the team of teachers, it wise for the curriculum director to carefully read though it to ensure that all content is being covered, that it is connected to expected student outcomes, and that biblical worldview development is as intentional and thoroughly integrated as possible.

A Final Note: Biblical Worldview and Spiritual Formation

In this chapter, the focus has been on the development of curriculum that leads to students more fully developing a biblical worldview. The monograph, however, is focused on both spiritual formation and biblical worldview development. It is my conviction that quality biblical worldview integration in the classroom is a critical component of spiritual formation.

We can think of spiritual formation as becoming like Christ and fulfilling the purpose for which God created us. Matthew 22:37–40 reminds us that we are called to reflect God's glory on this planet and to know Him, love Him, and love others with all our being. Spiritual formation is a process toward human flourishing. It is part of the redemptive process that is carried out by God's Spirit at work in and through us; it does not happen solely through human effort, nor is it something that "just happens" because we are Christians.

Teachers in a Christian school who intentionally prepare lessons using a biblical worldview integration approach will necessarily be influencing the potential spiritual formation of the student. For example, when students deal with uncomfortable questions arising in the curriculum, but explore a biblical answer to those questions, the external truth of God's Word is presented for their consideration and engagement.

In Romans 12:2, the apostle Paul reminds the Roman church that we are not to be conformed to the pattern of this world—that is, we are to not think as the world thinks. Our worldview is to be shaped or transformed by the renewing of our mind. This should be the focus of the teacher and the curriculum: to teach in such a way that students not only process information in their minds, but also are open to a change (through a renewed mind) to become more like Christ with each passing day. As they are informed by the Word of God, they realize that they can choose—and that the Holy Spirit can work through God's truth to reform our broken and sinful minds and hearts. Equipped with a biblical worldview, students think and act biblically as well as grow in Christlikeness, as they follow Jesus who was the Word made flesh (John 1:14). Both spiritual formation and biblical worldview development are not only related, but are also lifelong until we see Christ and we know as we are known (1 Corinthians 13:12).

When we desire for students to learn something, we intentionally plan for that learning to take place. It is no different with spiritual formation and biblical worldview development. The work of Christian educators, curriculum, and schools is to nurture students' ability to think and act biblically, now and in the future, and to cultivate in students an abiding love for God and desire to follow Him.

Biblical Worldview Integration Rubric

Created by Sandy Cassio for ACSI's Leadership University (reprinted with permission)

Component	Unsatisfactory 0	Basic 1–2
Using Lesson Content to Determine BWVI Statement	The teacher's plans demonstrate little understanding of **correlations** and **contrasts** between the lesson **content** and **biblical truths.** Erroneous, illogical, or nonsequitur connections are evident; the teacher may create an unrelated Bible study or devotion.	The teacher's plans demonstrate limited or partial understanding of **correlations** and **contrasts** between the lesson **content** and **biblical truths.** Limited, erroneous, illogical, or nonsequitur connections may be evident; limited unrelated Bible study or devotion may appear.
Writing BWVI into the Lesson Plan	No BWVI statement is written; or a BWVI statement uses an irrelevant Bible reference or analogy.	The teacher attempts to formulate a BWVI statement; the statement directly quotes one or more essential worldview questions and has little connection to lesson content and purpose.

Proficient 3–4	Distinguished 5–6
The teacher's plans demonstrate knowledge of **correlations** and **contrasts** between the **current lesson content** and **biblical truths.** Almost no evidence of erroneous, illogical, or nonsequitur connections; the teacher avoids creating an unrelated Bible study.	The teacher's plans demonstrate thorough understanding of **correlations** and **contrasts** between the lesson **content,** the scope and sequence of the **subject,** and **biblical truths.** No evidence of erroneous, illogical, or nonsequitur connections; the teacher avoids creating an unrelated Bible study.
The teacher formulates a BWVI statement that makes a **generalized** connection to (1) one or more essential worldview questions, (2) stated lesson purpose, and (3) the unit essential question.	The teacher formulates a BWVI statement **specifically and naturally** connecting the lesson plan to (1) one or more essential worldview questions, (2) stated lesson purpose, and (3) the unit essential question.

Component	Unsatisfactory 0	Basic 1–2
Communicating BWVI Purpose with Students	The teacher neither displays nor explains BWVI to the students.	The teacher displays the BWVI statement in the classroom (on a whiteboard, smartboard, slide, or poster) sometime during the lesson; the teacher orally announces BWVI when introducing the lesson purpose, but does not instruct on how the biblical worldview connects to the lesson content.
Incorporating BWVI into Discussion Techniques	The teacher makes no reference to the BWVI of the lesson during the instructional event.	The teacher makes vague reference to the BWVI statement during the instructional event. The teacher uses very few questioning techniques.
Using BWVI in Assessment	Assessment does not incorporate BWVI.	Assessment (whether formative or summative) loosely leads a student to recall **correlations** and **contrasts** between the lesson **content,** the scope and sequence of the **subject** and **biblical truths.** Assessment results cannot be measured or documented.

Proficient 3–4	Distinguished 5–6
The teacher displays the BWVI statement in the classroom (on a whiteboard, smartboard, slide, or poster) at the onset of the lesson; the teacher orally announces BWVI when introducing the lesson purpose, but gives little or only perfunctory instruction on how the biblical worldview connects to the lesson content.	The teacher prominently displays the BWVI statement in the classroom (on a whiteboard, smartboard, slide, or poster) at the onset of the lesson; the teacher orally announces BWVI when introducing the lesson purpose, giving explicit and thorough instruction on how the biblical worldview connects to the lesson content.
At some point during the instructional event, the teacher specifically reminds the students of the BWVI statement. Questioning techniques create limited opportunities for critical thinking and reasoning.	Throughout the instructional event, the teacher connects specific elements of the lesson to the BWVI statement. Dynamic, open-ended questioning techniques create opportunities for critical thinking and reasoning among the students.
Assessment (whether formative or summative) attempts to evaluate student understanding of **correlations** and **contrasts** between the lesson **content,** the scope and sequence of the **subject,** and **biblical truths.** Sometimes assessment results are measurable and documented.	Assessment (whether formative or summative) evaluates student understanding of **correlations** and **contrasts** between the lesson **content,** the scope and sequence of the **subject,** and the stated **biblical truths.** Assessment results consistently are measurable and documented, thereby informing the teacher of the effectiveness BWVI lesson planning and execution.

The Faculty Development Perspective: Training Teachers for Biblical Worldview and Spiritual Formation

Annie Gallagher

If Christian school faculty are qualified to teach and are Christians, do they need professional development in biblical worldview and spiritual formation approaches? To answer this question, let's consider Jesus, the Master Teacher, who provided professional development to His handpicked leadership team of twelve followers. These men worshiped in the Jewish temple and celebrated the Passover meal and other Jewish feasts with Jesus. Some worked alongside John the Baptist. Some were recognized for their strong faith in God. Yet even with their background, the disciples needed a growth plan with learning experiences and specific training in knowledge, attitude, and skills for the nuances of fulfilling the Great Commission and the Great Commandment. Jesus' professional development plan included three years of strategically planned events to train up future leaders. The expected outcome, or the mission, was to make fishers of men (Matthew 4:19, 28:19–20). This training was to prepare leaders to seek, teach, and save the lost (Luke 19:10, Mark 2:17), and equip others to do the same (1 Corinthians 11:1; 2 Timothy 2:2).

The background of the twelve is not dissimilar to the background of many faculty members. Faculty members might have a strong Christian testimony, attend church, and participate in Bible studies. However, can they articulate a biblical worldview and explain how to influence biblical worldview development and the spiritual formation of a child? Similar to the mission set for Jesus' team of twelve, the mission of Christian education "must have as its primary goals the salvation and discipleship of the next generation" (Schultz 2021, 28). Faculty members, as followers of Jesus, are also disciples with the mission to share the gospel message and make disciples through their vocation. Therefore, they need to learn how to positively influence the spiritual formation and worldview development of their students.

And just like in Jesus' example, faculty members need a well-designed path for continued training and development to fulfill the mission of Christian education.

The "How" of Faculty Training and Development

When a school leader or leadership team plans for professional development efforts, especially those related to biblical worldview development and spiritual formation, there are important steps to take. Planning professional development is a sort of reverse engineering process. One imagines and considers the final product or expectation and then takes it apart, bit by bit, to determine the necessary building blocks. Four of the key building blocks are as follows.

Set Goals

First, create a clear picture of the expected end goal by defining terms and describing the expectations. After presenting and promoting the goal in clear terminology, determine the subskills needed on the learning path and the instructional methods that will allow the subskills to be practiced throughout the professional development process. Finally, plan how the ideas, skills, and attitudes learned during training will be preserved as a "way of doing" biblical worldview development and spiritual formation at your school (Taylor 2018).

The desired expected outcome or set of outcomes needs to be articulated, presented, and promoted to keep every stakeholder focused and moving toward the same end. Schools that have well-articulated expected student outcomes or portrait-of-a-graduate statements that include spiritual maturity might find those useful in creating an ongoing professional growth plan for faculty in biblical worldview development and spiritual formation. The final goal is not achieved by what the teachers can do, but instead by how what the teachers do affects the students. Professional development includes activities designed to equip educators with knowledge, skills, and attitudes that, in turn, will improve student learning (Guskey 2002). Designing professional development plans for biblical worldview development and spiritual formation requires an understanding of the sequential hierarchy of concepts and skills needed to reach the expected outcome. What concepts, skills, and experiences do students need in order to influence their development of a biblical worldview and spiritual formation? What then do teachers need to know or be able to do in order to teach those concepts and skills and provide students with those experiences?

Finally, articulate these goals and the activities designed to meet them through the professional development plan. This plan creates the learning path for faculty which will ultimately affect the path of student learning. For example, if the expectation is for students to be able to read and comprehend what they read, the learning path for professional development needs to consider what the teachers and the students need to know and be able to do in order to meet the end goal. The path of professional learning, or the "how," is most successful when the plan scaffolds teachers from simple to complex, and from known to unknown. At the same time, the instructional methods and experiences used to grow teachers' knowledge, skills, attitudes, and spiritual maturity should align with best practices for adult learning. Professional learning is considered successful if the innovation becomes part of teachers' regular classroom practice or active repertoire.

Prioritize Relationships

"Be fishers of men" was the end goal of the three-year professional development plan implemented by Jesus. Jesus kept the goal in front of the disciples at all times. All learning experiences were provided to achieve the overall mission or learning goal. The learning experiences had to instill the knowledge, attitudes, and skills needed to cast the gospel message as a net and patiently wait to see if there would be a catch. Importantly, this required the disciples to know how to relate to all sorts of people, understand the human condition, and stand firm when encountering opposition. And most importantly, they had to not simply know about God, but needed to know Him intimately. Knowing God empowered them to cast the gospel net confidently and then sort the catch in order to identify who would be the next people to become disciples. All of the learning had to provide opportunities within personal relationships to observe, gain knowledge, and practice skills needed to achieve the end goal. Professional development plans for biblical worldview development and spiritual formation thus must incorporate a relational element.

Similarly, partnership principles (Knight 2007) will help move adult learners toward independent implementation of new ideas and methods. The partnership principles require that during professional learning all participants are treated with equal value, are given opportunities to dialogue about their opinions, and are able to make choices about their professional learning activities. Additionally, participants should have time for real-life practice and reflection on the skills and ideas they are learning. These principles are all evident in Christ's delivery of professional development.

Use Varied Approaches

Along these lines, the Master Teacher used a variety of instructional techniques to grow the future leaders' understanding, heart attitudes, and actions. Jesus modeled for the team members how the various aspects of the job were to be completed with thoughtfulness, humility, compassion, and intentional action. What was it that the disciples saw, heard, were taught, and experienced as they participated in His learning plan? The list is rich. They witnessed Jesus' teaching in the synagogues, preaching the gospel, healing, and casting out demons (Matthew 4:23–25, Mark 1:39). The disciples saw and personally experienced how Jesus conveyed the value of each individual in how He related to all sorts of people (Mark 10:13–16; John 4:27). The disciples were taught how to pray (Luke 11:1–4). Much was learned as the group spent time together building relationships with one another as they learned how to achieve the goal to be fishers of men.

Yes, instruction and information were sometimes provided directly to individuals and in small groups (Matthew 5:1–2; 7:28–29). At the same time, questions were posed to the team members to build reflective thinking about circumstances and context (Mark 8:27–29). These reflective questions fostered the disciples' ability to determine truth and appropriate responses. Jesus completed the professional growth plan by providing opportunities for practice; the disciples put into action what they had learned in terms of right thinking, attitudes, and skills as they were sent out in pairs to practice what they witnessed from Jesus (Mark 6:7–12; Matthew 10:1; Luke 9:1–7). Finally, after three years of Jesus' modeling, direct instruction, questioning, and guided practice, the disciples were ready to continue the mission on their own.

Consider Coaching

Jesus used a coaching model to provide a series of learning opportunities all focused on a single expected outcome that was understood by the disciples. The disciples were actively engaged in the learning process. Professional development for the disciples did not take place solely by "sit and get" methods of instruction, though there were certainly times when Jesus had His students sit and listen. Jesus taught with a balanced variety of instructional methods and in a sequence that was sensitive to the spiritual, emotional, and cognitive conditions of the disciples. And throughout the Old and New Testaments, many examples of coaching are evident—like Elijah and Elisha, Jethro and Moses, and Paul and Timothy. In these examples, one can see elements of modeling, questioning, and providing feedback with guided practice. Most of the biblical coaching examples included long-term and strategic efforts focused on clear expected outcomes. These efforts were successful because they were enveloped in caring and honest personal relationships.

Professional development provided through a coaching model leads to more frequent practice and skill with new strategies, more appropriate implementation, and longer retention of knowledge than through traditional methods of professional development (Joyce and Showers 2002; Knight 2007). What does the coaching process look like in practice? Bruce Joyce and Beverley Showers (1982), considered to be among the founding experts of peer coaching, frame the coaching process using the elements of teaching. Successful implementation of an innovation (defined as anything new to the learner, whether a new method, tool, or new term) is brought about through the following elements of teaching: 1) study of the why and what of the innovation; 2) demonstration of the innovation by an expert; 3) practice with the innovation while providing feedback in protected conditions; and 4) coaching one another to work the innovation into regular practice. When analyzing the course of professional learning provided by Jesus to the disciples, the elements of teaching are evident. Jesus articulated the goal, taught and modeled ways to achieve the goal, provided practice with feedback, and coached through relationship how to make their knowledge, attitudes, and skills become part of their everyday way of doing things.

The "When" of Faculty Training and Development

Discipleship and professional learning are ongoing processes. A workshop here or there will not suffice in helping teachers to develop their own worldview and related teaching skills. Research has shown that sufficient duration and frequency of professional development are key to teacher outcomes (Swaner 2016). So from the beginning of a training program, systemic processes ought to be established in order to preserve and build upon the result of the training. Support, accountability measures, and reflection opportunities are needed to continue and maintain professional growth.

Provide Support

Support comes in the form of planned collaboration time for faculty related to the desired outcome, a collection of resources, exemplars for teachers and administrators, and coaches who serve as resident guides for the new innovation. These kinds of support require both human and tangible resources, for which school leaders must plan and budget. Yet without these supports, efforts to train and develop faculty in these areas will ultimately fail to take root in the school's instructional culture. Ongoing support ensures that the school's investment in professional development, focused on biblical worldview development and spiritual formation, will pay dividends over the long-term.

Provide Accountability

Accountability occurs through the attention given to the continued implementation of the skills, attitudes, and experiences provided for students. Upon completion of the training program, two steps can be incorporated into the life of the school to foster continued accountability. The first step is to establish a timetable that stipulates the frequency of implementation with the expected outcomes and the corresponding time to reflect on the implementation. The second step is the use of criteria that paint a picture of the expected outcome and can be used to provide feedback. The timetable for implementation and reflection, along with the descriptive criteria, should be included as part of the practice phase of training to build the habits needed for full implementation and to build a common language to communicate expectations and feedback. Without support and accountability, the results of professional development efforts will soon fade away.

Provide Onboarding

Finally, onboarding is often overlooked as a requirement for preserving the thinking, attitudes, and skills learned during professional development. The teachers and administrators who completed the current professional development plan may do well with implementation, but what about the new hires for next year? How will they get up to speed with what other faculty members are regularly implementing? There are at least two ways to answer this question. First, abbreviated components of the professional development program can be included as part of the onboarding process for new teachers and administrators. Second, similar to a long-term learning plan for current faculty and administrators, a new teacher training program that takes place over several months or even the first two years has the potential to help preserve the school's instructional culture, while also applying best practices of professional learning.

The "What" of Faculty Training and Development

As you do the reverse engineering for biblical worldview development and spiritual formation, ask yourself, what do you want teachers and students to do related to a biblical worldview? What do you want teachers and students to demonstrate with spiritual formation? The following steps will help in answering these questions.

Define Terms

The answers to these questions require that the constructs of biblical worldview development and spiritual formation be defined. A definition of each needs to be first grounded in scripture and then articulated, presented, and promoted, so that all stakeholders have a shared understanding from which to develop practices. Both biblical worldview development and spiritual formation are lifelong processes that are influenced by one's surrounding community. With respect to a biblical worldview and spiritual formation, these constructs are similar and intertwined, but not the same thing.

A worldview can be described as a "pattern of ideas, beliefs, convictions and habits that help us make sense of God, the world, and our relationship to God and the world" (Noebel and Myers 2015, 10). A biblical worldview is one where a person's ideas, beliefs, convictions, and habits align with the Bible. It involves seeing and responding to the world as Christ would. Worldview assumptions are generally unconsciously held but affect how we think and live. Worldview reflects the academic and cultural community in which one lives and resides (Scott and Magnuson 2006). The beliefs, convictions, and habits that help us make sense of God, the world, and our relationships to God and the world are heavily influenced by the ideas we are exposed to and think about, the relationships we maintain, and the activities in which we engage. Biblical worldview development begins at birth and is influenced early on by interactions with primary caregivers. As a child grows, the weekly family routines, the nature of faith practices of others with whom the child interacts, and the exposure to ideas through literature, media, peers, and education influence and shape the child's worldview. In other words, worldview continues to be developed by one's academic and cultural surroundings (Cosgrove 2006, Smith 2016).

Spiritual formation for the Christian, on the other hand, is "the Spirit driven process of forming the inner world of the human self in such a way that it becomes the inner being of Christ himself" (Willard 2022, 12). Evidence of one's spiritual formation can be seen in three dimensions: the cognitive dimension, or thinking; the affective dimension, or relational; and the volitional dimension, or actions (Hollinger 2005). While spiritual formation begins and is matured by the work of the Holy Spirit, it is influenced by one's desire for transformation, the practice of spiritual disciplines, and a nurturing community of faith and love (Teo 2017, Willard 2002). Spiritual formation begins when the Holy Spirit convicts a person before salvation and transforms after salvation within a faith community and by the influence of God's Word (Willard 2002, Teo 2017). The Holy Spirit begins to shape a person from the inside to become Christlike. The Spirit's work moves more quickly if the person has an openness to transformation and seeks growth through God's grace.

It should be noted that the definition of these constructs varies even within Christian education. Therefore, although definitions are offered throughout this monograph and in the paragraphs above, it is important for Christian school educators to do the necessary study required for properly defining these terms for themselves and their schools. This process of study itself can be part of a development program for both leaders and faculty, as it will lead to deeper understanding of the concepts, which will in turn inform their practice.

Plan Holistically

As mentioned, biblical worldview development and spiritual formation both are holistic processes. The people and culture in which we live the moments of our day contribute greatly to how our spiritual experiences are interpreted and understood. Therefore, children's experiences in the Christian home, school, and church will nurture worldview development and spiritual formation by providing examples of what is valued in faith and how to do it (Fowler 1981; Scott and Magnuson 2006). Understanding how biblical worldview development and spiritual formation are shaped and influenced enables educators to take intentional steps to form a school culture that nurtures the shaping process. Thinking opportunities, relationships, and actions are strong shaping and influencing dimensions. So, it makes sense for educational institutions to promote opportunities for students to think critically about worldview ideas, build relationships with other Christ followers, and participate in experiences that provide guidelines and examples of Christlike living and draw them into a saving relationship with Jesus.

The three dimensions of thinking, relationships, and experiences can be simplified with the terms head, heart, and hands, respectively. Hollinger (2005) explains that complete faith involves thinking, spirituality, and mission or action. These dimensions nurture each other and are dependent on one another. They are not standalone entities. Complete faith is understood, felt, and lived out. These dimensions of faith align with the components of a worldview: beliefs, convictions, and habits. The head dimension is primarily a thinking aspect that centers on beliefs and understandings. The heart dimension includes affections, passions, and deep spiritual experiences that come through relationships and interactions with Jesus and others. The hands dimension involves actions or experiential activities.

Given the three dimensions of faith—head, heart, and hands— Christian schools can attend to these same dimensions when building a culture intended to shape students' worldviews and influence spiritual formation. Therein lies the definition and means for biblical integration. Biblical integration must be seen as a holistic shaping process that takes place through thinking, relationships, and actions. Biblical integration methods and models can consequently be classified according to their primary focus: to foster thinking habits, to build relationships, or provide application experiences. Again, it is important to remember that the three dimensions are not discrete from one another. However, sometimes it is necessary to focus teacher training for biblical integration more on one dimension—depending on what requires the most improvement, be it to develop the thinking, relational, or experiential learning opportunities for students.

It has been established that worldview development is shaped by ideas we think about, relationships with others, and experiences in which we participate. Spiritual formation is similarly influenced. Thus, the culture of a Christian school should promote and practice head opportunities for thinking about ideas presented in subject matter from a biblical perspective using biblically integrated instruction in the classroom. The culture should also promote and practice heart opportunities to build relationships with other followers of Christ, and Christ Himself through such programs as chapel, retreats, and small groups. In addition, the culture should promote and practice hands opportunities to participate in experiences that exemplify Christlike living such as service-learning (see chapter 9 of this monograph).

Putting It All Together*

Each school can examine its school culture to determine which dimension—head, heart, or hands—requires improvement. First, define what the end result of biblical worldview development and spiritual formation should look like. What will a well-functioning school culture that practices opportunities for thinking biblically, building relationships with Christ and others, and experiences that exemplify Christlike living look like? This end goal for each dimension needs to be clearly defined, not just talked about. Creating a visual picture of what each fully functioning dimension looks like will enable the school to communicate the criteria for success. The clear visual picture will also facilitate reverse engineering of the building blocks needed to create the end result, which include the concepts and skills needed, as well as specific training experiences that will provide direct instruction, modeling, guided practice with reflection, and coaching.

---

* To learn more about Transformed PD and the PAQ Method, a biblically integrated instructional approach designed to equip teachers to reveal Christ and worldview principles in every subject, visit https://transformedpd.com/the-paq-method/.

Part 3:
Programs and Practices

Teaching for Transformation (TfT): A Holistic Framework for Learning and Formation*
Darryl DeBoer

Christian schools are places of longing. The longing of schools themselves is to live into the promises of their mission and vision. The longing of parents is to send their children to Christian schools that shape learners within the character of Christ. The longing of Christian school leaders is to partner well with parents within the education journey of their children. The longing of students is to be engaged in meaningful learning experiences that recognize their identity as creative and unique image bearers of their Creator. And, finally, the longing of Christian school teachers is to be able to invite, nurture, and empower all learners, including themselves, within God's redemptive story.

Teaching for Transformation (TfT) has emerged out of the sum of these desires. At its core, TfT is a framework that equips Christian school teachers with practices and skills to design learning experiences that fulfill the longings of students, teachers, parents, and Christian school leaders. At its core, TfT urgently embraces the ongoing story of redemption that is playing out in real time within the classrooms of our Christian schools—God's Kingdom is "here and now." TfT roots both the learning (curriculum and competencies) and learners (teachers and students) in the immediacy of God's redemptive story. TfT acknowledges the need for the students to master the curriculum (it is school after all!). However, TfT centers the learning and the learners themselves within the reality that God is inviting us to participate with Him in the making of all things new again. God's Kingdom is at work and the purpose of learning, and the shaping of learners, finds its direction within this story of love and redemption. Thus, TfT helps teachers and students to "see the story."

Within this redemptive narrative, the purpose of fourth grade is not solely to prepare learners for fifth grade; the purpose of fourth grade is to

---

* This chapter appears also in *Teaching Redemptively*, 3rd edition, by Donovan Graham. See your.acsi.org/teachingredemptively for more information about this resource.

provide learning experiences that invite students to see God's story at work through fourth grade writing, reading, math, and physical education. Further, the purpose of fourth-grade is to provide opportunities for the students to participate in God's story—right here, right now—as they study science and social studies and as they play at recess. There is important Kingdom work to be done right now by these fourth-grade image bearers. In fact, there is redemptive work that is specialized for these fourth graders, and TfT equips teachers to design learning that is rooted within this truth and invite students to be active within the story of redemption—to play their part. Thus, TfT helps teachers and students to "live the story."

As often as we receive the message that the purpose of schooling is to prepare students for life after school (and there is a reality to this statement), our Christian schools' mission and vision statements reveal a deeper purpose of schooling. As James K.A. Smith (2009) passionately shares in *Desiring the Kingdom*, "What if education, including higher education, is not primarily about the absorption of ideas and information, but about the formation of hearts and desires?" (17–18). The challenge is that Christian school leaders, parents, teachers, and students live within these dueling purposes of Christian schools: the mandate to cover the curriculum and the mandate to form hearts and desires. The struggle is real. Talk to any Christian school teacher and you will hear about the challenge of teaching within these dual understandings of the nature of school. Often this manifests in questions like, "How do I find the time?" or, "How do I cover the curriculum and engage the heart?" or, "How do I assess that?" The competing stories of educating a student for life after school, while simultaneously inviting students to play their part within God's redemptive story, is ever present within our Christian schools, and our Christian school teachers feel the tension most deeply.

The tension of these competing stories reveals the second driving force behind the development of TfT: Christian schools need a framework for their teachers to be successful in their desire to teach within the promises of their school's mission and vision, within the redemptive story—while at the same time, engaging the curriculum. So, as much as TfT has emerged out of a longing for formational Christian education, it has also been born of necessity: Christian schools need to support their teachers with practices and tools to teach in such a way that the redemptive promises of the school's mission and vision can come alive within the primary task of a Christian school. This chapter will provide a high-level overview of TfT's design, beginning with the central "Deep Hope" and then moving into the three core practices of Storyline, Throughlines, and Formational Learning Experiences (see Figure 1 below).

Figure 1: Teaching for Transformation Overview

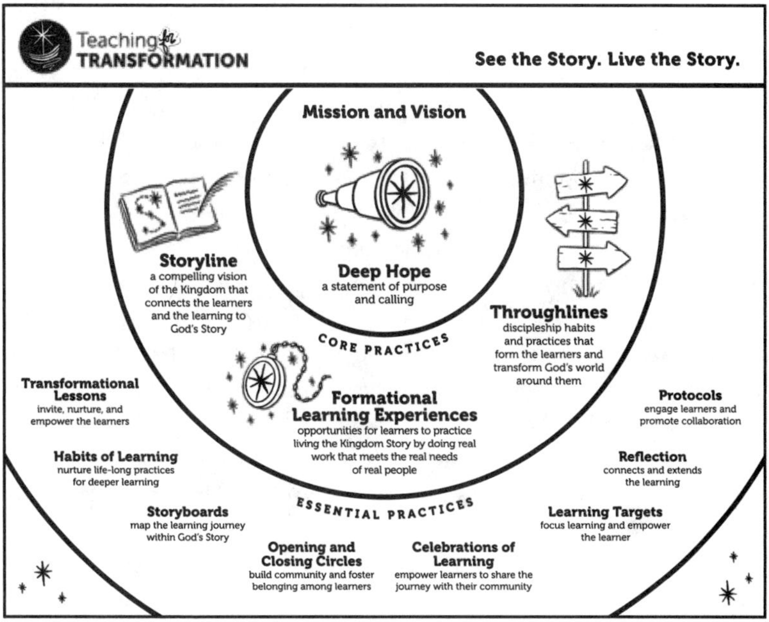

Deep Hope

TfT begins with Deep Hope, is sustained by Deep Hope, and moves toward Deep Hope. Centering TfT within Deep Hope is a reminder that every Christian school originates from a collective Deep Hope, with articulated mission and vision statements that explicitly name their Deep Hope. Parents' Deep Hope for their children motivates them to send their children to Christian schools. And let us not forget that these students themselves also have a Deep Hope for their lives. It is not an understatement to recognize that teachers have classrooms brimming with Deep Hope students, sent by their Deep Hope parents, to attend Deep Hope Christian schools.

The Deep Hope of TfT is to invite, nurture, and empower God's image bearing teachers and students to join Him in His redemptive work of making all things new again as they learn together within our Christian schools. Within the TfT framework, a Deep Hope is an articulation of how the teaching, learning, classroom environment, and curriculum aligns with the intended purpose of God's created world. It is a statement that recognizes that the end goal of Christian education is to participate in God's redemptive work.

TfT explicitly invites teachers to root their work within their Deep Hope for their teaching, students, and classroom space. Within the TfT framework, the very first question that teachers ask themselves as they launch their classrooms and begin to design learning experiences is, "What is my Deep Hope for …. ?" Initially it may begin as broad as, "What is my Deep Hope for ninth-grade science this year?" It may gradually take on more specific forms like, "What is the Deep Hope for my learners within this ecology unit?" and, "What is the Deep Hope for our watershed field work?" Within the context of the ninth-grade science class, a Deep Hope explicitly places the learner, the teacher, the curriculum, and the learning journey within God's redemptive story. Teachers' Deep Hopes remind them to design learning experiences that invite students (and themselves) to see God's story at work and to play their part as ninth-grade scientists within this story.

Beginning with Deep Hope is a significantly different starting point from traditional (competing) starting points for planning a year or unit, such as, "What science curriculum do I need to cover?" or even, "What is the next chapter in our science textbook?" These are more common starting points that reinforce a competing purpose of schooling: to cover the curriculum and of course these questions need to be addressed; however, a learning journey that begins with, "What is the Deep Hope for my learners within this ecology unit?" takes a different path (and ends in a different place) than a learning journey that begins with the question, "What is the content I must cover?" If we believe Christian education to be distinct, the Deep Hope as a starting and end point is one way to authenticate this distinctiveness.

Inviting teachers into their Deep Hope is also an act of hospitality. It is an opportunity for teachers to articulate who they have been created to be and it is an invitation for them to root their teaching and their calling within God's redemptive story. It is a reminder that they, and their teaching, are consecrated and dedicated to the service of God. Their teaching is their own personal and professional fulfillment within God's story. For many, it serves as a reminder as to why they were attracted to Christian education in the first place. And, yes, they will also cover the curriculum.

Deep Hope is also an invitation to move from fear into freedom. Teachers and students are free to play their part in God's story—they are free to be who God intends them to be. This freedom nurtures inclusivity because a Deep Hope recognizes all students as God's image bearers and invites all to play the part within God's story within the classroom. While content and pedagogy inherently are at risk of excluding some learners, a Deep Hope rooted within the redemptive story invites all learners to participate in the Kingdom story. Teachers and students are free to question, free to engage, free to create, free to be in relationship, free to fail, free to grow, free to learn, free to be made whole, and free to release fear. Deep Hope invites grace, nurtures grace, and empowers grace.

And through it all, the Deep Hope serves as teachers' North Star as they design learning experiences for their students. The North Star establishes the destination: it guides, corrects, and redirects the learning journey, and it reassures students and teachers of their identify and purpose in Christ. A Deep Hope is different from a plan, even though it results in a plan. Deep Hope guides daily decisions, both big and small, that are made within the classroom. A Deep Hope provides a means of feedback for the teacher's plans and decisions, as administrators and teachers alike can ask questions like, "Does this align with our Deep Hope?" and, "Will this move us closer to our North Star?" The Deep Hope helps to discern what is essential, what is distracting, and what competes with God's redemptive story. And just as the North Star lies beyond our reach, so too is the Deep Hope beyond our limits. Deep Hopes are deep and big and wide—in fact, too deep, too big, and too wide to be realized on one's own. Deep Hopes require prayer and are an invitation for the Holy Spirit to partner with us in the learning journey, in the story of redemption. Without prayer, without inviting the Holy Spirit, and without purposeful teaching, Deep Hope is at risk of becoming hopeless.

Deep Hope paints the beautiful picture of the destination and simultaneously becomes the launch of the learning journey. After articulating a Deep Hope, TfT roots the Deep Hope within core classroom practices that will nurture and empower the Deep Hope—Storyline, Throughlines, and Formational Learning Experiences—which are meant to nurture the Deep Hope of any classroom.

Teaching for Transformation Core Practice: Storyline

To walk into a classroom that is being shaped by the practices of TfT, one of the first things you would notice is the classroom Storyline. Simply stated (yet so complex!), the purpose of Storyline is to explicitly connect the learners, curriculum, and learning experiences to God's redemptive story. The classroom Storyline reveals God's redemptive story—it ensures all "see the story." Thriving classroom Storylines have three main components: significant language that forms the tagline, ongoing rhythms and practices in the classroom that connect to the Storyline, and classroom visuals that illustrate how the Storyline connects the learning and learners to God's story.

Imagine that Storyline stands with two outstretched arms. One arm stretches and tightly grasps God's story; this story names God as Creator of all things and all that is good and beautiful and delightful. However, sin has entered this good and beautiful world and things are not as they were intended to be. Yet, through the sacrificial act of Jesus on the cross, darkness and brokenness have been defeated and we are all invited to play our part in the making of all things new again. And with the other outstretched arm, the Storyline grasps the learning experiences. Within this posture of tightly holding both God's story and the learning, the Storyline brings these two together into a symbiotic relationship that simultaneously amplifies both God's story and the learning experiences within this classroom. The Storyline engages two ongoing essential questions that will impact the learning:

- *Question 1: What does the learning within this class reveal about God and His story?* So, within the context of this question and a ninth-grade science class, the study of ecology reveals that our Creator God desires and creates systems that are ordered, sustainable, relational, balanced, and beautiful. The study of ecology reveals that God's creation, including humans, flourishes within order, balance, and relationship. And, when ecosystems exist within their intended order, there is beauty and flourishing for all of God's creation. A functional Storyline will ensure that this ninth-grade ecology unit will be about more than ecological principles.

- *Question 2: How does God's redemptive story orient the learning and learner within the curriculum?* Storyline empowers the students to engage the question: "How now shall I live?" Within the learning sequence of "What? So What? Now What?" the question of "What?" is answered by the curriculum, but "So What? Now What?" is answered by God's story. Staying within the example of the ecology unit, as participants in God's story, students are called to discover how broken relationships disrupt order and balance ("So What?") and are invited to participate in the restoration of God's created order so that all of creation can flourish as their Creator intended ("Now What?"). To play our part within God's story, our students are invited to identify activities that threaten the sustainability of ecosystems, they are invited to live sustainably, and they are invited to play their part as ecology students in restoring the order, balance, and disrupted relationships within these ecosystems. It is through God's invitation to participate with Him in the making of all things new again (His redemptive story) that this unit on ecology finds its meaning and purpose.

With a living Storyline, teachers can ensure that these two distinctly Christian questions drive the learning within any unit. Storyline will empower teachers to counter the competing narrative that teaching is about covering the curriculum. Without a Storyline that is constantly pulling the learners and learning into God's story, a teacher's Deep Hope is at risk of becoming unwarranted hope. So, teachers choose language for their Storyline tagline that mirrors their Deep Hope. Once a Storyline's tagline has been identified, teachers design rhythms (repeating opportunities for students to connect their learning to God's story) that keep the Storyline (and, therefore, God's story) living within the classroom. These liturgies that connect learning to God's story via the Storyline shape the culture of a classroom, and the culture forms the people. The liturgies that sustain the Storyline create the vision of the good life for the teacher and the students. Within the ecology unit, the learners are nurtured within the vision of the way it was intended to be, and as we grow in our desire of this good life, we begin to actively pursue that which supports this vision of the good life.

As teachers and students live into Storyline rhythms, the learning begins to generate relics and visual cues that begin to fill the classroom space, through artifacts that demonstrate that this classroom is a learning space where's God's story is alive in the here and now. These artifacts combined with Storyline language and rhythms continue to shape the learner and the learning with God's story. The little stories of learning within this classroom are connected to God's big story and the learners are playing their part within this story. Storylines create structures to make God's restoration story evident within the learning of our Christian schools. A Christian school full of thriving Storylines becomes an embodiment and testament of God's redemption story. At the same time, if Storylines reveal the kingdom of God, they are equally able to reveal competing stories—those that erode the kingdom of God. Storylines rooted in God's story reveal competing stories that exist within the curriculum, classroom practices or whole school culture. For example, competing stories promote the glory and gains of self while simultaneously eroding Kingdom stories of blessing and renewal.

Living Storylines sustain Deep Hope. Storylines become a plot for the Deep Hope to weave and thrive, and a story's plot requires characters—the students and teacher—to play their part within God's restoration story. Within the setting of the Christian school classroom, the plot of God's story takes root, and the students and teacher are invited to explore their role and to take on their character within the story. So, who are these characters within God's story and what role are they to explore? The TfT core practice known as Throughlines explores this question.

Teaching for Transformation Core Practice: Throughlines

While Storyline connects the learner and learning to the story, Throughlines invite roles that the characters can play within this story of redemption. Throughlines simultaneously reflect Jesus and invite postures of grace to permeate learning experiences. To live redemptively is to invite and nurture grace; to live as a servant worker, environment keeper, justice seeker, etc. is to embody the grace that characterizes those playing their part within God's story (see Figure 2).

Figure 2: TfT Throughlines

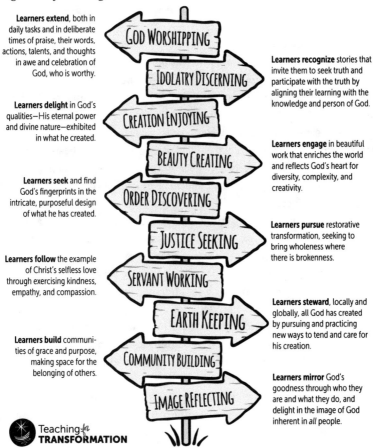

Learners extend, both in daily tasks and in deliberate times of praise, their words, actions, talents, and thoughts in awe and celebration of God, who is worthy.

Learners delight in God's qualities—His eternal power and divine nature—exhibited in what he created.

Learners seek and find God's fingerprints in the intricate, purposeful design of what he has created.

Learners follow the example of Christ's selfless love through exercising kindness, empathy, and compassion.

Learners build communities of grace and purpose, making space for the belonging of others.

Learners recognize stories that invite them to seek truth and participate with the truth by aligning their learning with the knowledge and person of God.

Learners engage in beautiful work that enriches the world and reflects God's heart for diversity, complexity, and creativity.

Learners pursue restorative transformation, seeking to bring wholeness where there is brokenness.

Learners steward, locally and globally, all God has created by pursuing and practicing new ways to tend and care for his creation.

Learners mirror God's goodness through who they are and what they do, and delight in the image of God inherent in *all* people.

GOD WORSHIPPING
IDOLATRY DISCERNING
CREATION ENJOYING
BEAUTY CREATING
ORDER DISCOVERING
JUSTICE SEEKING
SERVANT WORKING
EARTH KEEPING
COMMUNITY BUILDING
IMAGE REFLECTING

Teaching *in* **TRANSFORMATION**

Like Storylines, Throughlines also must connect to classroom learning experiences. Within the context of learning, Throughlines are discipleship habits and practices that both form the learners and transform God's world around them. Throughlines assist students, teachers, and parents to imagine what it means to be a disciple within God's story; they guide how students are to live the story while learning within it. Throughlines both identify and form the character of the those living redemptively within God's story.

Throughlines are an invitation for students (and their teachers) to claim their identity in Christ. They provide an opportunity to counter the common educational narrative in which students might be seen as their accomplishments or their failures—such as the grades they receive (the narrative of if they don't do well, they are poor students) or the teams they play for (the narrative of if they win, they are good athletes). Throughlines provide a vision of discipleship for students' identity within God's story— such as servant workers, idolatry discerners, community builders—and who they can continue to grow to become. It is essential that Throughlines not be merely seen as labels (i.e. beauty *creator*, community *builder*), but as a way of living that can be practiced and strengthened (i.e. beauty *creating*, community *building*). We become servant workers by practicing servant working. We become community builders by practicing community building. By practicing these ways of living, we grow our desire to become these ways of being; we are being formed. As James K.A. Smith (2013) shares in *Imagining the Kingdom*, "The focus on formation is holistic because its end is Christian action: what's at stake here is not just how we think about the world but how we inhabit the world—how we act" (12). Our loves and desires can be cultivated and our hearts oriented by practicing ways of being that are consistent with the kingdom of God.

The formational strength of the Throughlines is realized by living into the action that accompanies Throughlines: building, working, seeking, discerning, and so forth. Both teachers and students see the story they are part of and grow in their desire to live consistently and redemptively within this story, by practicing and acting out these Throughline ways as they learn. Within the ongoing example of the ninth-grade ecology unit, students are provided learning experiences that both teach the curriculum while also providing opportunities to practice Throughline ways of being. Students learn about food webs (curriculum) *and* practice creation enjoying (Throughline). Students learn about nutrient cycles (curriculum) *and* practice order discovering (Throughline). Students learn about resource management (curriculum) *and* practice earth keeping (Throughline). The combination of the core practices Storyline (see the story) and Throughlines (live the story) ground the learning experiences, and learners, explicitly and deeply within God's redemptive story. A deep grounding in God's redemptive story is precisely the Deep Hope of the teacher, parent, and Christian school. God's story is no longer for later or "out there;" God's story is at play right here in science class and the teacher, and students are actively playing their redemptive part in this story. Storylines and Throughlines bring the teacher's Deep Hope to life.

A collective set of Throughlines provides common language for teachers that span grade levels and subject areas and becomes a key mechanism for the traditional silos and fragmentation of school to be broken down. Integration and inclusivity naturally follow the implementation of Throughlines as all learners are invited, nurtured, and empowered to claim their Throughline identity in their entire Christian education journey. The promises contained within the school's mission and vision are alive within classrooms that provide opportunities for Throughlines to be practiced.

The final core practice of TfT, Formational Learning Experiences, ensures that the learners are given the opportunity to practice a Throughline way of living while also magnifying a student's motivation for, and engagement with, the learning.

TfT Core Practice: Formational Learning Experiences

TfT teachers share that Formational Learning Experiences (FLEx) are very disruptive. If we are honest, it is fair to say that most hours of typical school days, students are at their desks involved in a variety of tasks that aim to transfer knowledge from the teacher, textbook, or assignment to the student. Once knowledge has been transferred, the student is given opportunity to complete tasks and eventually demonstrate the learning (or lack thereof) back to the teacher. In fairness to our dedicated Christian school teachers, most of our Christian schools were built on this factory model of schooling—our teachers are simply working within the context of the schooling model Christian education adopted. FLEx disrupts this model: learners are empowered to demonstrate learning by playing their redemptive roles within God's story beyond a worksheet, beyond a test, and beyond the walls of their classroom and Christian school. FLEx is disruptive.

FLEx provides opportunities for students to be shaped by God's story through learning with and from people outside of the classroom, while participating in work that is having a redemptive influence in the community in which we live, while simultaneously mastering the curriculum. Teachers design learning experiences in which students engage in "real work that meets real needs for real people" and quite often this means that students need to either invite the world into their classroom or leave their classroom to go into the world so that they can deepen their learning and live the redemptive Kingdom story. *Real work* refers to redemptive work as articulated by the Throughlines: servant working, image reflecting, God worshipping, etc. *Meeting real needs* looks like students addressing brokenness or amplifying wholeness within the realms such as beauty, truth, order, justice, and sustainability. And *real people* refers to those who participate with the students during these formational learning experiences: experts who guide and provide feedback for the students, organizations who partner with the students, and those who need to learn of or from this important redemptive work.

Within FLEx, students in every grade are given the opportunity to respond to God's call to be active, restorative, and creative in God's story of redeeming love. Sometimes students will address brokenness, but, at other times, they will amplify the redemptive work that is already happening. It is through the practice of engaging in meaningful schoolwork and redemptive work within the community that the learner is forming a compelling vision and desire for living within God's story. Student learning is also deepened as purposeful schoolwork generates increased engagement, motivation, and mastery of content. Impacting God's world requires good learning! Addressing real needs for truth, beauty, sustainability, and justice within the community develops lifelong learning skills such as joy-filled collaboration, gracious communication, curious thinking, and courageous problem solving. FLEx are opportunities for Christian schools to provide students alternative motives beyond good grades and individual achievements. FLEx moves students beyond compliance and invites them into learning experiences that recognize and honor them as the unique image bearers that they are, and their schoolwork is offered as worship to their Creator God.

FLEx also amplifies the TfT core practices of Storyline and Throughlines. Storyline invites learners to see God's story not just in the classroom, but also outside of the school. FLEx ensures learners get to interact with both. While Throughlines invite the learners to practice discipleship ways of being, the formational potential of Throughlines is limited if students can only practice them within the classroom. For example, there are justice seeking or earth keeping opportunities within a classroom; however, there are greater needs and opportunities for justice seeking and earth keeping outside of the classroom or the school. By practicing Throughlines in the community, students are proclaiming the arrival of the Kingdom and demonstrating what the kingdom of God is about. Without the disruption of FLEx, there is the possibility that students will only *talk* about the Kingdom in Christian education, but not have the opportunity to *participate* in the formation of the Kingdom—and therefore not be fully formed by the Kingdom. Along these lines, it is important to note that personal formation is not restricted to the students—FLEx also shapes the teacher. Teaching for transformation is a result of teaching *from* transformation.

It is important to note that inviting students to engage the world in redemptive work beyond the classroom feels risky to most teachers. It is common for teachers to feel vulnerable as they invite students into FLEx; there are many uncontrollable pieces of a FLEx, the outcome never fully certain, and the learning journey provides many twists and turns that need to be handled within the moment. But, within this liminal space exists the transformational possibility of the Holy Spirit to enter the learning process. Further, the teacher is also presented the opportunity to both extend and receive the hallmark of redemptive work: grace. Thus, FLEx provides the opportunity for the Deepest of Hopes for Christian education, which is only fully realized in true partnership between teachers, students, and the community.

Putting It All Together

TfT classrooms and schools not only live out their Deep Hopes through Storylines and Throughlines, but also employ pedagogical practices that are likewise story-oriented, purposeful, and engaging. These include a set of eight essential practices:

- *Storyboards*, which map the learning journey within God's story;
- *Learning Targets* that focus learning and empower the learner;
- *Transformational Lessons*, which invite, nurture, and empower the learners;
- *Protocols*, which engage learners and promote collaboration;
- *Habits of Learning* that nurture lifelong practices for deeper learning;
- *Reflection* to connect and extend the learning;
- *Opening and Closing Circles* that build community and foster belonging among learners;
- *Celebrations of Learning* to empower learners to share the journey with their community.

While an in-depth exploration of these is not possible in this chapter, it can be readily seen that the TfT classroom and school is a place of deep engagement in meaningful and collaborative learning.[**] These practices enable teachers and students to participate fully in the redemptive story at the heart of the Christian school.

Christian schools are places of Deep Hope, and these Deep Hopes appear in a variety of forms—school mission statements, parents' decisions to send their children to a Christian school, a teacher's faithful response to answer the call of teaching with a Christian school, and a student's desire to belong and to be known. Whatever form in which the Deep Hope manifests, it is the most powerful starting place for a learning journey into God's story. TfT launches learning from Deep Hope. From there, it supports Christian schools and teachers in designing learning that invites, nurtures, and empowers students to play their part as they explore God's world through their learning. Through TfT, teachers and students alike come to "see the story, live the story."

[**] Visit TfT's website, www.teachingfortransformation.org, for numerous examples of TfT in practice within the classrooms of the TfT Network of Schools.

At the Intersection of Faith and Learning: The Harkness Approach
Justin Smith and Kim Fullerton

The Westminster Shorter Catechism (2020) asks the question, "What is the chief end of man?" The answer, "to glorify God, and enjoy him forever," clarifies the driving purpose for believers distinctly made to reflect the image of God and be in joyful relationship with Him. Similarly, the first question of the Christian educator should be, "What, then, is the chief end of Christian education?" At Little Rock Christian Academy (LRCA) in Little Rock, Arkansas, the answer is, "forming students in knowledge, wisdom, and virtue." If this is our chief end, then our next question should be what teaching and learning processes help us most strategically reach these ends. A key pedagogical approach at LRCA is the Harkness method.

The Harkness Approach
In 1930, Principal Lewis Perry of Phillips Exeter Academy and philanthropist Edward Harkness designed a form of student-driven pedagogy that deeply engaged students in their own learning. In a letter to Perry, Harkness wrote:

> What I have in mind is teaching boys in sections of eight . . . where boys could sit around a table with a teacher who would talk with them and instruct them by a sort of tutorial conference method, where the average or below average boy would feel encouraged to speak up, present his difficulties, and the teacher would know ... what his difficulties were .... This would be a real revolution in methods.

And indeed it was. Exeter is now one of many independent schools that use the Harkness method of teaching and learning to develop in students the habits of mind ripe for the twenty—first century: depth of knowledge, interpersonal skills, and the emotional intelligence to read and respond to peers and instructors. At LRCA, Harkness is an approach to spiritual formation and biblical worldview development that gives students the opportunity to think deeply, gain wisdom, retain knowledge, form a measured mind, and care for one another.

LRCA has been practicing the Harkness method in seventh through twelfth grade for six years. While Harkness gives teachers great data about the learner, perhaps more importantly, it gives students insight into their own learning journey—socially, spiritually, and academically. LRCA faculty value Harkness as an instructional practice because it offers the opportunity for students to think deeply and dialogue with others about eternally significant things, whether that be in math, French, English, or biblical worldview classes. Though other practices, such as the Socratic method, offer similar advantages, the prominence of the student voice in Harkness distinguishes it:

> Students sit facing one another in some version of a circle and then discuss the text, looking for meaning and connections. The teacher acts as facilitator, guide, and coach and discussions typically ebb and flow: a question, a response, a pause, a connection outside the classroom, more questions and so on. Unlike teacher-centered instruction, this method of student-centered teaching [is] designed to capture the imaginations of students, challenge them to grapple with complexity, and create a space where they can refine their thoughts on things ranging from literature, scripture, historical documents and theology to scientific discoveries. (Smith 2018, 10–12)

Faculty at LRCA have found that through the Harkness table, students have grown in their abilities to connect new and previous learning and retain information learned in class. They also learn to disagree with others thoughtfully and respectfully. But most importantly, Harkness proves an immensely valuable pedagogical tool when it comes to the intersection of faith and learning.

Faith, Learning, and Harkness

By engaging students in dialogue and questioning with texts and one another, Harkness requires students to form, present, defend, and amend their thoughts, opinions, and convictions. Within the context of the Christian school, this process is harnessed to hone the biblical worldview of students, as well as develop students' capacity for biblical thought and action.

At LRCA, we have identified four specific ways that Harkness practices amplify spiritual formation for our students. First, the emphasis on student voice reminds them of their value as image bearers designed to be in relationship with our Creator and with others. The table provides a great place for students to practice using their voice, to learn patience, forgiveness, and repentance, and to build confidence and skill as speakers and listeners.

Second, Harkness reinforces the value of asking meaningful questions and seeking application outside the classroom—reminding students that their lives are purposeful, that they are destined to contribute good things to the post-Fall, broken world we inhabit. Third, it affirms students' roles as keepers and speakers of truth to one another and to the lost. The table provides a safe place for students to test competing truth claims and bolster their own faith. And finally, it teaches students how to journey well as individuals and as part of a community.

Coming to the Table

At LRCA, we regularly host workshops for Christian school faculty who are interested in learning the Harkness approach and implementing it in their own schools. While this chapter is not a similitude, we do want to offer a glimpse of how Harkness works at LRCA through the eyes of our faculty. In the eight faculty narratives that follow, you will notice in more than one instance students practicing the "one anothers" of scripture, along with gaining confidence as listeners and communicators.

Old Testament, Ethics and Culture, Fundamentals of the Faith
(Anthony D. Davis, Ph.D. Computer Information Sciences)

On the day of Christ's resurrection, Luke depicts two disciples on a journey. On the road to Emmaus, they struggle with events that took place over the past three years leading up to the ultimate event of Good Friday. Along the way, Jesus—albeit in hidden form—discusses scripture with Cleopas and his friend until they reach their home. They finally come to the table where Jesus breaks bread with them, culminating in the "aha" moment of Christ's true identity.

In the biblical worldview classroom, Harkness discussions often parallel the journey of the disciples—at the daily level and over the course of the semester or year. As Luke's narrative suggests, Jesus saw merit in allowing the disciples to discuss and struggle with the events and information concerning scripture. On the road, He questioned them and allowed them to express their thoughts on the events, their thoughts on scripture, and their interpretation of what happened. He then guided them through scripture to show the true purpose of the events and information they struggled to make sense of. This process continued until they came to the table to break bread. Then … the light bulb goes off and they both see the true identity of the Messiah! It is worth pointing out that only after the journey did they realize the true meaning of the events and who Christ is. They needed the journey.

As Christian educators, our students typically come to the table with knowledge of scripture, but like the disciples, they too struggle with understanding events that took place in historical context and what they mean for the world today. Harkness provides a way for our students to experience a "Road to Emmaus" journey where they discuss and, many times, struggle with ideas. As educators, we are to walk alongside them on this journey, assign appropriate materials for discussions, and use the Word to guide them in the truth. Harkness discussions provide a valuable tool to help students arrive at "aha" moments during individual classes, but the table also allows space for the Holy Spirit to open their eyes and, like the disciples on that journey, acquire a burning heart for Christ. Just like the disciples, they too need a place to journey toward Truth.

Inquiry in Worldview Frameworks, Apologetics, Old Testament
(Loren Rugen, B.A. Biblical Studies)

The tricky thing about worldview is that it isn't limited to strictly fact-based knowledge. Rather, it is an umbrella term for the complex interplay between knowledge we already have, our current assumptions about how the world works, and experiences that either confirm or disconfirm those assumptions. Therefore, the methodology to teach students about how to grow and self-reflect in worldview terms must be multifaceted. In essence, Harkness offers practice in skills requisite for such growth. As we know, it is only when students try a skill via independent practice that the content becomes their own. Specifically, there are two types of skills that immediately come to mind for most Harkness discussions: learning how to *ask* and learning how to *answer* meaningful questions.

It is rare for students to initially exhibit a growth mindset when encountering a difficulty they perceive as above their mental "pay grade." Instead, they default to what they already assume (this is especially true in worldview-oriented material). This is detrimental for growth as it tends to reinforce stereotypes, misconceptions, and ignorance. And this is where the art of asking quality questions comes in.

Many students assume that asking questions is a sign of stupidity. On the contrary—it cannot be stated enough that genuine, quality questions are a sign of intelligence! It may not be the kind of knowledge-based intelligence that already comprehends the ins and outs of the subject at hand. Rather, it is the curiosity-type of intelligence willing to wonder, seek, and find. The whole point of being a student is that one doesn't know the things that need to be learned. In short, questioning is a prerequisite to growth. And, as educators, we realize it is a skill which must be taught and practiced. Harkness discussions help students hone this skill.

Case in point: one day we were wrapping up a discussion by reviewing questions the students had submitted for homework. One student commented that he felt stupid for asking his question since the answer seemed so obvious now after the discussion. After a moment of reflection, I replied that the answer only seemed obvious now because he had asked the question first. You see, the whole point of asking a question is not because you already understand, but because clarification is needed for deeper understanding. You won't be looking for the answer until you are willing to develop and ask a good question. Yes, the quality of the questions might improve over time, but that is the whole point. Students have to start somewhere before they can improve. The more questions they ask about other perspectives, and the more questions they encounter about what they believe, the better prepared they will be to go deeper into important worldview issues.

In summary, students need face-to-face interactions where they can learn the essential skill of asking and receiving questions. Whether it is to work collaboratively to understand a difficult concept or to hash it out over a controversial issue, the application of those skills in the context of Harkness discussions are invaluable for worldview growth.

9th Grade New Testament and Life of Christ
(Suzanna Dudley, B.A. English and French)

Imagine a large, round table, similar to a dining room table, that takes up the majority of a room and seats a close-knit group of thirteen teenagers. When my students walk into class on the first day, the Harkness table forces them to break the discomfort of looking at one another and begins creating a culture of vulnerability, where asking hard questions and listening to one another's viewpoints is a given. Using the three strategies below, I have been able to create this classroom culture, leading to great learning around the table.

Starting with circle questions. At the beginning of almost every class, I ask students a question that each is required to answer, including me. Circle questions range from silly questions like, "Do you put milk in your cereal first or cereal then milk?" to more thoughtful questions like, "What is a high from your week and what is a low?" Consistently having circle questions, especially at the beginning of the year, makes my students comfortable to speak and builds the foundation for future conversations on spiritual topics.

Getting out of the way. When I separate myself from the table, sit at my desk, and choose to listen for a designated amount of time, students do the heavy lifting. This is often when I experience the "magic" of Harkness where students become more professional in their communication and come away with deeper reflections on the content. I grade on a rubric and often have designated topics I require them to address in the discussion. But, I find that students are more willing to ask out-of-the-box questions and are more likely to grapple with challenging questions for longer periods of time when I "get out of the way." Even though the room is small, removing myself from the Harkness table prompts them to own the discussion more than when I am seated with them.

Curating challenging content and reflection. My classes do not shy away from challenging topics or content, even in ninth grade. The Harkness discussions on content from the book of Revelation and on topics about heaven, sexual sin, and why God created us male and female, have been the richest discussions with powerful learning moments. However, to get there, students must do pre-work to prepare for the discussion. I take a grade for their pre-work, and then I "get out of the way" and let students grapple.

After the discussion, students reflect as a class with questions like "How did we do on making sure 100 percent of voices were heard?" Afterward, students independently write a reflection, which might include follow-up questions stemming from the discussion or a spiritual reflection on how the topic connects to them and their spiritual life.

Although I am often not at the table during the actual Harkness discussion and am instead tracking and making notes, I have found that creating a healthy class culture, using pre-Harkness work, curating challenging content, and incorporating a reflection after the discussion bring students to powerful learning moments.

8th Grade English and Creative Writing
(Hope Winburn, M.Ed. Reading)

My first introduction to the illustrious Harkness table was as a student at Phillips Exeter Academy. I remember the fear and doubt that consumed me as I walked into my eleventh-grade classroom. After much prompting, I finally summoned the courage to speak during a discussion. My teacher told the other students to write down what I had said, a moment I will never forget. What a gift, to make someone feel significant. When I reflect on why I became a teacher, it always comes back to this moment. I want students to know their voice matters, I want them to feel confident in their ability to express their ideas, and I want them to practice compassion by considering multiple perspectives. For me, the most effective instructional tool to accomplish these goals remains Harkness.

Many students have gone from intimidated to inspired while sitting around the oval Harkness table. Through practice, students become more comfortable and adept at testing theories, making claims, using evidence to support their ideas, making biblical and real-world connections, and asking insightful questions. The value of Harkness is that students have a safe environment to practice these skills before they will need to use these same skills in their future jobs and relationships. They have a chance to learn from their peers and Christian educators in order to solidify their beliefs before those very beliefs are challenged after they graduate.

Additionally, Harkness is an exercise in humility. Harkness encourages students to explore a variety of ideas and to try to see beyond their own thinking. It is important for students to acknowledge that their thoughts on a topic or text are not the only ideas that exist or are correct. My favorite question to ask students after a Harkness discussion is what insightful comment they heard a peer make, because it encourages them to reflect on what knowledge they gained from the discussion that they would not have captured on their own.

The productivity of a Harkness discussion is often determined before the discussion even begins. So much of the student's ability to meaningfully contribute depends on their level of preparation prior to discussion. Students can be better prepared for Harkness when they are discussing a text they are familiar with, when they are given questions ahead of time, when they bring original questions to the discussion, and when they set personal goals based on feedback and rubrics from previous discussions. Students grow when they reflect on their performance from previous discussions and take ownership of the overall quality of the class. One of the most powerful moments is when students genuinely cheer on the contributions of their peers, rather than only focusing on the next comment they want to make. While learning how to share their ideas is important, the ability to truly listen to others is just as, if not more, important. As a student, Harkness offered me the gift of confidence. As a teacher, I hope Harkness offers students the gift of compassion.

AP Language, Senior English, Concurrent Oral Communications
(Jennifer Byrd, M.A. English)

Planning, questioning, and frequency. Having practiced the Harkness method for five years, I am convinced these three factors are key for a successful Harkness experience with students. As an English teacher, our discussions always center around a text. So, pre-Harkness activities, such as having students develop questions, give them something specific to bring to the table. Additionally, I typically have them discuss the reading in small groups for five to ten minutes before our large group discussion. This allows them to learn from each other and also get over their nervousness. During this time, each group has an assigned outcome, such as writing at least three questions on the board. This bit of structure helps students feel more secure and willing to bring their ideas to the table with confidence.

Recently, after learning about Arthur Costa's levels of thinking and questioning, I have focused on helping students write higher quality questions. In Costa's model, Level 1 is inquiry, Level II is analysis, and Level III is application. In the past, I've noticed my upper-level students tend to spend too much time on application (sometimes to cover for the fact that they didn't do the reading!) This year, I've tracked the time that each class has spent on each level, with the goal of spending 60 percent of the conversation analyzing the text. We always begin with inquiry and usually end with application, but I stress that analysis is the most valuable aspect of the discussion. Learning about levels of questioning and how to apply them to discussion has been a rich experience for me as a teacher and is bearing fruit for the learners.

Finally, frequency is key to helping students gain confidence in Harkness. Some students are intimidated by large group discussions. My biggest mistake in the past was the infrequency of the practice. I would have one or two discussions per quarter, and they would each be worth a test grade. This year, I've tried to schedule a Harkness discussion every week, and they've been worth a quiz grade. This maximizes habituation and minimizes stress. If students do not score well on one discussion, they have six to eight more chances before the end of the quarter.

In my classes, we have a goal of 100 percent participation for each discussion. Another technique is to recruit students to help pull more reluctant contributors into the conversation. As a result of increased frequency and decreased weight of grades for each Harkness discussion, I've seen more participation and less stress in my students this year over previous years. Planning well, teaching students to form quality questions, and helping them gain confidence lead to valuable outcomes in student learning around the Harkness table.

Introduction to Romance Languages, French I, Advanced French
(Tony Saegert, M.A. French)

My first experience with Harkness left me feeling conflicted. Philosophically, this method of learning, which facilitates student-to-student engagement, aligned with the communal environment I aspire to create in my classroom. However, Harkness discussions seemed to tackle such abstract ideas, that I couldn't envision what it might look like in my French classroom where students are learning basic vocabulary and grammar. Giving it more thought, I came up with more questions than answers and could have easily walked away to return to "what worked." Nevertheless, just as I would encourage my students to embrace the tension as part of the growth process, I chose to remain open to the method of Harkness.

Over the course of the next months, my understanding of Harkness was continually refined and expanded through readings, observations, and practice. "Do I have to use text? Who creates the questions? Can I contribute? How do I even begin to grade this?" Answers to these questions revealed that Harkness is not so much a science, but rather an art that can be tailored to each teacher's style and strengths. Regardless, it became evident that no matter how one executes the discussion, a commonality among all Harkness tables was the notion of learning through collective discovery. Personally, this realization unlocked how my premature understanding of Harkness as simply abstract discourse could be adapted to teach the skills of my French curriculum.

Prior to implementing Harkness, instruction in my class would have predominantly consisted of me, the teacher, presenting content to my students. Often I would write verb conjugations on the board that students would then memorize. In contrast, Harkness invites the learner into the process by drawing out their own wonderings. Using a short text, students are challenged to voice what they notice, such as a pattern of every word after *"vous"* ending in "-ez." Collectively, the class hypothesizes the grammar concept in play and then attempts to apply it in a new context. How rewarding to witness students assume ownership of their learning!

In addition to this shift, Harkness in a different language has provided students with valuable opportunities to practice communication skills such as asking clarifying questions, actively listening, and maneuvering around breakdowns in comprehension. Though their knowledge of the French remains the primary focus, I am confident that the supplementary skills gained through Harkness will long outserve their ability to rattle off *"je ne sais quoi."*

UCA College Algebra, UCA Statistics, AP Statistics
(Cheryl Rowen, M.S. Statistics)

When high school leadership first shared their vision of using the Harkness method in each subject area, I could not reconcile adding to what seemed like an already full curriculum. Harkness in math? Immediately my mind went to asking, "What would I have to give up to make room for the inefficiency of large group discussions?" Thus began my journey of trial and error in how to capture the learning benefits of Harkness in a math classroom. Here is a snapshot of what you might see were you to walk into my math classroom these days.

To begin, let's note the environment. Students are sitting at tables in groups of two to three. These tables can be pushed together for larger or whole group discussions as well. The room has whiteboards on multiple walls to allow students to write out their ideas. Though I might teach a mini-lesson briefly setting up necessary skills to dive deeper into some real-world problem, I rarely lecture. Instead, I roam, stopping intermittently at each group, prompting students through a series of questions, challenging their answers or perhaps encouraging them to continue down a line of reasoning. When asked, "Is this correct?" I might say, "Would you put that solution on the board? Let's discuss it!"

At first, students are frustrated, hesitant even, wanting to be "right" before they show their work to their peers. But after two or three weeks together, I can see this beautiful transformation take place. They become owners of their learning. They find their "math voice," and with increasing confidence put up their work in what we call a "white board critique." They lean on each other, rather than on me as the "authority" for confirmation. While students might occasionally sit around a large table to discuss topics such as, "is using a calculator considered cheating?" you'll more often see smaller groups of students working on problem sets or up at a white board discussing and presenting multiple methods of problem solving to their peers.

My deepest desire as an educator is to inspire students to apply questioning, research, and logic not only to defend their own faith in Jesus Christ, but also to share His love and redemptive story to the world around them. Of course, our student outcomes indicate that we desire that "LRCA graduates … are confident calculators, creative problem-solvers, and clear communicators in mathematical language," but using math to show our students the very nature of their Creator, His predictability, His precision, and the order in which He created all things, including math, is my utmost priority. Asking questions such as "Did you know that God was the first to carry out a census?" (Numbers 1:2), or using probability logic to test the likelihood of one man, Jesus Christ, fulfilling two or three prophecies just by chance (thus juxtaposing chance occurrence against logical evidence to show the intentional design of the gospel story), teaches our students to view all learning—even math—through a biblical lens. The type of thinking, questioning, collaborating, listening, and risk-taking that Harkness learning requires, prepares our students to move from just "doing" math to "applying math" in their world, in their own voice. Their math voices become powerful when tied to the heart of faith.

A Journey Worth Taking

As Christian adults, a short reflection on our own sanctification process reminds us of how we have grown: in knowledge, in understanding, and in practice. We are not who we were (praise the Lord!). Harkness is an educational practice that takes into consideration what it means to be human. The skills practiced in Harkness discussions, crafted and scaffolded by intentional, loving Christian educators, help students live out their identity and their purpose.

Using Harkness as an instructional practice has been a worthy pursuit on our campus. We continue to see flourishing and good growth in our students, and it is an important tool in our mission to shape hearts and minds evermore into the image of Christ: in knowledge, wisdom, and virtue. Teachers and students would agree that, messy and unpredictable as it can be at times, applying Harkness as an instructional practice is a journey worth taking.

Bringing Worldview and Formation "to Life": Service-Learning in Christian Schools

Lynn E. Swaner and Roger C.S. Erdvig

Christian schools are places where teachers and students engage the timeless truth of the Bible and its implications for the academic disciplines, for our meaning and purpose, and for living well together. Christian schools are also communities in which spiritual formation and personal growth occur in the context of relationships. As such, Christian educators do not stop at students' "knowing all the right answers," but rather desire that students' hearts, minds, and habits be transformed by knowing the God of truth, ultimately extending His restorative work to their homes and communities.

This is a worthy goal that requires serious thought about the implications for Christian teaching and learning. James K.A. Smith (2009) explains, "a Christian understanding of human persons should also shape *how* we teach, not just *what* we teach" (33, emphases in original). How can we design teaching and learning in Christian schools in a way that recognizes the authority of scripture and the power of the Holy Spirit, and takes its direction from the Great Commandment (Matthew 22:37–39), the Great Commission (Matthew 28:16–20), and the Cultural Mandate (Genesis 1:26–28)?

In our thirty years of collective experience and research in the Christian school setting, we have found service-learning to be a powerful approach in this regard. Service-learning is well-suited for engaging students, maximizing their learning, nurturing their personal growth, developing their worldview, training them to serve others, and equipping them to live out Ephesians 2:10: "For we are his workmanship, created in Christ Jesus for good works, which God prepared beforehand, that we should walk in them."

Defining Service-Learning

Service-learning is a pedagogy that connects classroom learning with service opportunities in the community, in an iterative cycle where student learning is facilitated through structured reflection. There is significant evidence from research that service-learning has a positive impact on a range of student outcomes. Beyond greater mastery of content and course-specific learning goals, service-learning has also been shown to elicit multidimensional change in students, including positive impact on overall academic achievement, commitment to civic engagement, formation of beliefs and values, growth in leadership competencies and personal development, and a lasting commitment to serving others (Berson and Younkin 1998; Astin, Sax, and Avalos 1999; Vogelgesang and Astin 2000; Felten and Clayton 2011; Warren 2012; Furco and Root 2010; Eyler and Giles 1999; Prentice 2007; Radecke 2007). While this research was not conducted in Christian schools, this list of positive outcomes closely reflects the vision and mission statements of many Christian schools.

At its essence, service-learning is a pedagogy that connects classroom learning with service opportunities outside the school. Service-learning is one of several types of "experiential learning" methods, but it is unique in that "students engage in activities that address human and community needs together with structured opportunities intentionally designed to promote student learning and development" (Jacoby 1996, 5). Stanton, Giles, and Cruz (1999) point to the name "service-learning" as providing its definition, by joining "two complex concepts: community action, the 'service,' and efforts to learn from that action and connect what is learned to existing knowledge, the 'learning'" (2). Because of this, the "hyphen in service-learning is critical in that it symbolizes the symbiotic relationship between service and learning" (Jacoby 1996, 5).

We have identified four widely accepted characteristics of service-learning through our work with schools, research on student outcomes, and reviews of the literature. Service-learning as a pedagogy:

1. Connects community service or outreach with classroom learning and the curriculum;
2. Takes students outside of the school setting to do "real work that meets real needs for real people" (a phrase found in Teaching for Transformation, as described in chapter 7);
3. Creates authentic, meaningful relationships between students and those being served; and
4. Increases and enhances student learning, as well as students' desire and ability to serve others.

In addition to these four characteristics, we've also found it useful to

118

define service-learning by examining what it is *not*. There are four common educational activities that are not service-learning, but that are often confused with it. These are:

1. Community service or outreach with no linkage to the curriculum (including required community service hours);
2. Service that does not take students into the community outside of the school (e.g., clean-up projects around the school grounds or peer tutoring at the school);
3. Active learning without a direct service component, or that has no significant personal contact with those being served (such as creating a video, website, etc.); and
4. A one-time event, as opposed to sustained, multiple contacts with those being served (e.g., Christmas caroling at an assisted living facility).

All of these activities are certainly worthwhile, and we do not suggest that they are inconsequential. However, they cannot be linked through research to the same high degree of influence on learning outcomes as we have seen with service-learning. Indeed, in our qualitative focus groups and interviews with students over the years, they've told us that what they learned in class "came alive" through service-learning.[*]

Service-Learning, Biblical Worldview, and Spiritual Formation

All people and the institutions we populate (including Christian schools) are all situated in God's great and enduring story as told through the metanarrative arc of the Bible. Garber (2014) draws upon Augustine to explain:

> [H]uman beings are story-shaped people, stretched between what ought to be and what will be. In our imaginings, our longings, at our best and at our worst, we are people whose identities are formed by a narrative that begins at the beginning and ends at the ending—the story of scripture itself, of creation, fall, redemption

---

[*] This phrase informed the title of our book on service-learning in Christian schools, *Bring It to Life: Christian Education and the Transformative Power of Service-Learning* (Swaner and Erdvig 2018, Purposeful Design Publications).

and consummation …. It is a long story, and a complex story, and it is our story. (202)

Service-learning enables students—as God's image bearers, each with a unique design—to play a part in bringing God's redemptive work to the world, which manifests His presence and makes known His eternal purpose for humanity. The same can be said of the Christian school, as service-learning can become a vehicle for schools to engage intentionally in restoration work in their communities.

We can explain this better by starting back at the beginning, in creation, when God created Adam and Eve in His image (Genesis 1:26–27). As God's image bearers, people were created to be "very good," with abilities (or gifts and talents) that were to be used to cultivate and steward creation. As Donovan Graham (2009) explains, "The calling and task of humankind as originally decreed by God has never changed" (103). People today are still engaged in creating, cultivating, developing, growing, and learning, even if the object of their activity is not relationship with and worship of the Creator. The Christian school's role is to recognize that students are created in God's image and can be active players in God's redemptive plan as described in Ephesians 2:10. Service-learning gives students real opportunities to develop their skills and abilities (academic, relational, vocational, and so forth), to cultivate their worldview, and to engage productively in God's appointed good works.

The sharp turn from Creation to the Fall of humanity brought sin and death into the world. The Fall is the reason there is widespread suffering, pain, and need in the world. Service-learning enables Christian school students to see this brokenness in the world firsthand. Certainly they can see it many other places (whether in their homes, neighborhoods, on the news, or in their own hearts). The beauty of service-learning is that the educative power of the Christian school is brought to bear on students' view of fallen reality through direct exposure and reflection—mediated by Christian teachers who can serve as mentors and guides in the process.

Service-learning offers the chance for students to not only recognize and understand the brokenness they encounter in the world, but also to realize that the only solution is the redemptive work of God. In the biblical narrative, we recognize Jesus was the only one who could help us in our broken state. It was entirely because of God's initiation through the Incarnation, and His work on the cross, that we have access again to God and to true life (John 10:10b). Graham (2009) provides a powerful picture of God's redemptive work and its implications for the lives we are to live as believers:

> God did not sit back and say "how awful, but that is just the way it is." Neither can those who seek to reflect who He is .... We can readily see that our calling will not allow us simply to be content with souls that are saved and personal behavior that is ethical. God Himself identified with His people and came to them to live in their presence. The incarnation is a marvelous lesson in how we are meant to live out the image of God in the current age. (105)

Graham outlines several ways that "our behavior as redeemed image bearers should make a difference in the culture" (104) including bringing *healing* by addressing "the economic conditions that produce suffering [and] the social conditions that produce isolation and loneliness" (104); being agents of *renewal* by "taking something that already exists and making something better of it ... [like] renewal in our cities, housing projects, corrupt governments, and industry that has so little concern for its workers" (104); working for *deliverance* of others, as "redemptive activity should remove us and others from the bondage prevailing in the kingdom of darkness ... poverty, drugs, sexual immorality, racial oppression" (105); advocating for *justice*, to "right those wrongs precipitated by the fall, especially those we inflict on one another" (105) wherever we may find them; and seeking God's peace, or *shalom*, that "reflects the wholeness and togetherness God intended" (105), whether in caring for the environment as part of God's creation or caring for others around us (105).

The power of service-learning for the Christian school lies in its capacity to engage students in all of these redemptive activities. Teachers and students can use four key questions as they think redemptively about developing service-learning projects: What is missing in our community that I can create? What is good that I can cultivate? What is broken that I can cure? What is evil that I can curb? (Erdvig 2020).

Ultimately, service-learning can develop a biblical worldview of suffering and orient students toward a lifetime of restorative work on behalf of our God who is Creator, Savior, Sustainer, and Redeemer. Service-learning helps students to grow as ambassadors of Christ, who can make a difference in the fallen state of their communities and neighborhoods. Through this process, students can come to see their true purpose in God's story, and how they have been uniquely created and gifted by Him as active participants in that story—creating what is missing, cultivating what is good, curing what is broken, and curbing what is evil.

Despite the powerful scriptural basis for engaging students in redemptive service, we have found that Christian educators can sometimes be wary of educational methods that they perceive as originating from secular philosophies. We would counter that in the case of service-learning, the importance of serving others is a pervasive principle in scripture. This is supported by the example of Jesus' own teaching, as He used a variety of methods to instruct His disciples. These include:

- Direct teaching on serving (itself diverse, involving didactic instruction and parables);
- Reflective questions (e.g., in Luke 10:36, when Jesus asks an expert in the law to reflect on the story of the good Samaritan: "Which of these three, do you think, proved to be a neighbor to the man who fell among the robbers?");
- Modeling (washing His disciples' feet);
- Guided practice (such as the feeding of the 5,000 in Luke 9:12–17); and
- Unsupervised practice (sending out of the disciples out to serve others in Luke 9:1–6, 10).

We can say confidently that Jesus taught and practiced these approaches well before modern-day educational philosophers realized their power for learning.

The Service-Learning Cycle in Practice

Service-learning is a dynamic pedagogy that is an iterative cycle as opposed to a linear process. In the cycle of service-learning, students modulate between *classroom* learning and *service experiences*, with *reflection* mediating learning between the two (see figure below).

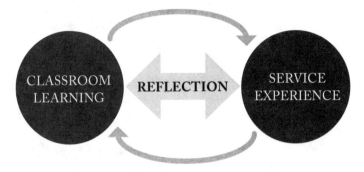

Classroom learning involves all of the course content and processes by which students engage that content (e.g., lessons, readings, assignments, and assessments). Ideally, service-learning is tied to course content throughout the academic year, rather than linked to a single unit or lesson. This not only expands the opportunity for student learning, but also serves to integrate service-learning more thoroughly in the curriculum. We do not mean to suggest that every class period is spent on topics related to service-learning; however, the competencies and knowledge students will need in preparation for the service experiences themselves should be incorporated regularly throughout the course. Additionally, it is important to provide students with instruction on the biblical basis for service. Service-learning should not be an add-on or extra work, either for students or for teachers. Ideally, service-learning should be fully integrated into the curriculum. This means that service-learning should be planned, implemented, and assessed as intentionally as any other part of the academic program.

Next, *service experiences* are opportunities for students to engage in meaningful service in the community outside of the school. Service experiences bear some similarities to field trips when it comes to logistics (insurance, permission slips, scheduling, transportation arrangements, budgeting for costs, etc.). However, service experiences differ significantly from field trips in terms of their purpose and format. The purpose of service experiences is to address real needs of the community partner, as *defined by that partner*. Needs to be addressed, as well as the ways to address them, are negotiated between the school and the service site. This partnership is what makes service-learning fundamentally different from charitable or philanthropic work (which tends to be unidirectional and non-relational).

Service-learning helps students develop humility in service, as Christ demonstrated when He washed the disciples' feet (John 13). It also fosters authentic relationships, where community members feel valued as true partners. Thus, students in service-learning need to have ample opportunity to develop relationships with those being served. For these reasons, service experiences are in sharp contrast to the "one-off" approach for most field trips; rather, students should have a sense of personal investment in the work of, and with, the community partner. Selecting sites for service that are near the school can help promote sustained relationships and break down community-school barriers.

Finally, *reflection* is an ongoing activity of thinking about and documenting personal experience and learning. Reflection mediates—or provides the connective tissue—between classroom learning and service experiences. More than merely summarizing or reporting on accomplishments, reflection is "a vital and ongoing process in service-learning that integrates learning and experience with personal growth and awareness" (Kaye 2004, 11). As students consider their personal experience via structured reflection throughout the entire service-learning project, they are practicing higher-order thinking skills and learning to become more self-aware.

Reflection can take many different forms, including journaling, guided discussion, creating artwork or poetry, and so forth. Reflection opportunities should be structured in such a way as to move students in an age-appropriate and developmentally consistent manner toward higher levels of integrating their learning from the classroom and service experiences. Because of the importance of reflection to service-learning, faculty should intentionally incorporate reflection activities into lesson planning for service-learning. Reflection opportunities can't be left to chance any more than a trip to a service site can be unplanned.

Service-Learning Examples

In practice, we have seen service-learning happen in every grade level and anchored in nearly every subject. We've also seen a tremendous range of community sites for service-learning, including homeless shelters, literacy centers, nursing homes, Christian ministries, community gardens, health clinics, and local churches. The possibilities for service-learning are limited only by the creativity of the faculty, students, and community partners involved. To help spark readers' imagination, we share an elementary and a secondary example here (many more examples can be found in our book, *Bring It to Life: Christian Education and the Transformative Power of Service-Learning*).

Elementary Math

An elementary teacher chose to implement service-learning in conjunction with the math curriculum, targeting the specific unit of graphing. The teacher reasoned that linking math concepts to service-learning would not only help students to master these concepts but also enable them to learn how to serve others and solve real-world problems at the same time. The teacher went through the curriculum and swapped out existing examples and sample problems with ones that related to addressing the unmet food needs of the community. The teacher utilized the outcomes that had already been identified in the course's curriculum guide (relative to the specific math units being targeted), as well as drew upon the schoolwide expected student outcomes related to academic excellence, biblical servanthood, and personal growth in students' gifts and talents.

The teacher reached out to a local food pantry to partner in a service-learning project. The food pantry—which had a large distribution network throughout the surrounding towns and county—relied on donations from individuals and corporations to meet the significant community need for free groceries, due to a high unemployment rate and cost of living. The class made four trips (one each academic quarter) to the food pantry, with the purpose of inventorying their supplies and identifying changes in supply and demand over the year. Parents were welcomed on this trip and many attended as chaperones. The students returned to class, analyzed the data together, and created reports for the food pantry. Also during these trips, they assisted with warehouse chores and interacted with food pantry staff, who discussed their work and the community needs. The class also participated in two distribution days, one in the fall and one in the spring, during which they assisted the staff and volunteers in handing out food to community members.

In order to deepen and cement learning, the teacher required students to keep a biweekly journal in which they responded to assigned reflection questions. These questions asked students to identify connections between their classroom learning and their service experiences, as well as reflect on how their work at the food pantry was helping them to grow in their unique gifts and talents, develop Christlikeness, and help restore and repair brokenness in the world through service. This further connected students' learning in both math and the service-learning project with the fourth-grade ELA and Bible curricula, thereby helping students to further integrate their learning during the year.

High School History

An eleventh-grade history teacher integrated service-learning into the curriculum on world history, by focusing on the concept of war throughout time. The teacher wanted the class to not only learn about war throughout human history, but also to gain a full appreciation of the great sacrifices and losses inherent in war. An important part of the course was discussing moral questions related to war—including exploring biblical views on the morality of war (debating whether and when war is justified)—and discussing ways that Christians should respond to the human needs created by war. In addition to the outcomes identified in the curriculum guide for the class, these larger questions helped to shape the desired service-learning outcomes.

The teacher's home church had a thriving veterans' ministry, headed by the community pastor. The ministry held monthly veterans' breakfasts at the church that were well attended. As a service experience, students assisted in preparing and serving the veterans, breakfast at the church four times during the year (once per quarter). During the breakfasts, students also sat at tables with the veterans and had opportunity to dialogue with them about their experiences. In addition, the students themselves developed and led several fundraisers throughout the year, including bake sales and a 5K race, to raise money for the veterans' ministry. They also assisted with local Veterans Day parade preparations and even marched alongside the veterans in the parade.

Students kept a weekly journal in which they responded to structured reflection questions provided by the teacher, many of which focused on students' views of war and how Christians should respond to the needs created by war. Students were required to read each other's journals and reply constructively to at least two other students' journals every week. In addition, after each service activity, the teacher spent the next class leading discussions to debrief students' experiences and connect what they learned to the curriculum. Students described their interactions with veterans as putting a "human face and voice" on the course content and the larger moral questions they were exploring. A culminating paper in the last quarter synthesized students' learning from the year. Finally, students created group projects in which they designed their own programs for meeting veterans' needs at their own churches. They presented these projects to the class and invited the community pastor in charge of the veterans' ministry to attend and offer encouragement and constructive criticism.

Implementing Service-Learning

Once Christian school educators grasp the potential value of service-learning to fulfilling their school's mission, they often are eager to get started right away. But service-learning requires intentionality, forethought, planning, and collaboration. Ultimately, successful planning will help teachers and schools to realize the promise of service-learning through successful projects.

Start with the Curriculum

It may be tempting to begin thinking about service-learning by dreaming of all the wonderful ways students can get out into the community to help others. The difficulty with this approach is that typically one of two things results: a project that focuses too heavily on service, and does not connect directly or strongly enough to the curriculum; or a project that involves active learning and student engagement, but that fails to incorporate reflection or authentic service adequately. Service-learning is a dynamic pedagogy that involves many moving parts (in terms of people and sites of learning), and it is difficult to assemble those parts into a successful service-learning project without careful thought.

The best place to start searching for service-learning ideas is in the *curriculum itself*, with the reason that service-learning projects must be grounded in the existing learning objectives, as well as the scope and sequence of courses. Service-learning works best when it naturally flows from the content being taught as opposed to being forced into the curriculum. A good way to start is for teachers to examine their course content and identify units, topics, or themes that may benefit from a more active learning approach and/or learning experiences outside of the classroom. Sometimes these can be areas with which students have difficulty in the course or that could use revamping after many years of being taught the same way. Some reflection questions to ask of the curriculum include:

- Which themes, units, and lessons have obvious practical, real-world applications?
- What content in this course could better be grasped by students if it involved hands-on learning?
- In what professions would a person use the themes and content of this course?
- How might God use a theme or topic in this course to meet people's needs?

In answering these questions, it is also important to consider what assignments, activities, field trips, and other course elements could be "swapped" with service-learning. This is because service-learning won't work as an add-on, as it is too time- and resource-intensive to simply wedge into an already packed instructional schedule. Moreover, for it to be meaningful for students, service-learning needs to be an integral part of their experience in the course. Thus, teachers need to not only think of where to anchor service-learning in the course content, but also how they will make sufficient room for it during the year.

We've also found collaboration to be extremely helpful in this initial stage of planning. For example, many times when we've led planning sessions with small groups of teachers they served as sounding boards for one another, by bouncing ideas back and forth until they begin to crystallize. As individuals share ideas about areas of their courses that may be taught effectively through service-learning, they can gain clarity and new insights through the questions and input from colleagues. It's not uncommon for ideas in one discipline or content area to spark new ideas in other areas. As their ideas develop, teachers can work in pairs or small groups to begin recording their thoughts and developing actionable plans.

Identifying Community Sites

The next step in the planning process is to identify sites in the community that may have needs suited to the project idea. This task can be daunting for many reasons, and teachers often start out fearing they will not be able to find a community site where their students can serve. Sometimes finding appropriate service sites can be a challenge, especially if the Christian school does not regularly engage with the broader community in which it is situated.

Often a good place to start is to connect with a local church. Many local churches will have significant outreach ministries that may be able to connect a teacher and class with legitimate community needs. For example, some churches operate food pantries, senior citizen programs, ministries to single mothers, or various ministries to at-risk youth. Most areas of the United States also have independent parachurch ministries that focus on specific populations, such as rescue missions, crisis pregnancy centers, and youth mentoring organizations. These faith-based organizations can all be good places to identify a need that can be met through a service-learning project.

However, it is wise to also consider choosing service sites outside of church and parachurch settings, as doing so can connect the school and students with the local community in unique and powerful ways. Local governments, chambers of commerce, Rotary Clubs, libraries, and other community organizations are all potential sources of information about needs that may work well for a service-learning project. Parks commissions, animal rescue organizations, and nature conservancies are also good sites to consider. Contact with local chapters of veterans' organizations, chambers of commerce, and other community or civic organizations may provide leads. In some cases, local businesses, medical offices or centers, nonprofits, and legislators' offices may be engaged in charitable or volunteer activities, which could be parlayed into service-learning projects for school students. The benefits of partnering with these kinds of organizations are many: students gain experience serving outside of the church, interact in meaningful ways with people who are often not believers, and learn how to engage in God's restorative work as an ambassador of Christ to the world.

It's important for teachers to be well-prepared for an initial conversation with a potential site, even if the site is well-known to the teacher. Preparation includes being clear on what the teacher is asking for and being realistic with what a project might look like. We've found that leaders in organizations generally enjoy connecting with youth and children, but they often cannot accurately picture what a successful service project might look like. Keeping in mind the value of establishing relationships with people (and not just doing a quick one-time service project), a good place to start is to ask them what ongoing needs they have and if they would be open to a discussion about how a group of students from the school may be able to help them. Explain the heart behind service-learning and how the purpose is to help students connect meaningfully with the community, while meeting real community needs.

Asking questions about logistics (what the students will do, how often they can visit, and with whom will they interact) is important, with the goal of determining whether or not the site is actually a good fit for students. The site needs to be chosen with realistic expectations of what the students can actually do, as well as what they are allowed to do (legally or otherwise). We know of a few situations where teachers went to great lengths planning a significant project, only to find out that the site they had in mind couldn't actually accommodate their students for legal, insurance, or space-related issues. Some simple investigation prior to in-depth planning can help to avoid potential lost time and disappointment.

Involving Students

To maximize the value of service-learning, teachers should avoid coming up with a fully developed project that gives students little opportunity to have a voice in planning and decision-making. While it is virtually impossible in a K–12 environment to give *all* planning over to the students, teachers should actively look for every opportunity to involve students in the decision-making process about what to do and how to do it. The older the students are, the more voice and responsibility they should have in planning their service-learning experiences. Thus, teachers in the upper high school grades will involve students in planning to a greater degree than in lower elementary, but all teachers can give some responsibility over to students—with the result that leadership skills can become an outcome of service-learning.

Support from Leadership

Service-learning, whether being implemented in one classroom or across an entire school, requires both innovative teachers *and* supportive school leaders. Besides the vision casting and philosophical support that must come from school leadership, there is a very practical side to successful service-learning to which leaders must attend. This includes tasks like securing funding for projects, ensuring faculty have time for planning, and providing ongoing support while projects are being implemented. It is not enough for school leaders to simply give their "blessing" to service-learning. Rather, teachers will need significant support across these and other areas for their projects to be successful. We have compared service-learning to a yearlong field trip, replete with all of the permission slips, bus logistics, insurance paperwork, and other details that can bog teachers down. Administrative support (through a part-time service-learning coordinator or existing office staff) can go a long way in helping teachers bring their service-learning plans to fruition. Finally, leaders can also support teachers with developing assessment plans, to determine whether and how service-learning is having a significant and positive impact on student learning, the school as a whole, and community needs.

Whenever we talk with Christian school leaders and teachers about mission and vision, we're met with enthusiasm and commitment for the work to which they are called. At the same time, we often hear that leaders and teachers are hungry for practical and effective strategies for pursuing their school's mission in the educational activities that make up the bulk of what they do. Service-learning can be just such a strategy. When teachers are committed to taking classroom learning into the community and school leaders support that commitment, students' engagement with course content can be significantly deepened. But beyond improved learning outcomes, service-learning supports the very core of Christian schools' missions—to nurture Christlikeness, biblical worldview formation, and the capacity for redemptive action in our students.

LEADING INSIGHTS: Biblical Worldview and Spiritual Formation

Reflection Questions for Leaders and Teachers
Cindy Dodds

This section of reflective questions will assist school leaders and their teams engaging in critical, culture-building conversations so that school practices consistently reflect the school's philosophy on biblical worldview and help to nurture the spiritual formation of both staff and students. The questions are categorized around the important elements of any Christian school's culture and practices: the school's mission and vision; leadership; school policies; curriculum development and pedagogy; internal relationships; social and cultural engagement; and external relationships. After discussing the questions with your school team, commit to action steps that emerge from areas of need, or efforts that can be strengthened, in regards to biblical worldview and spiritual formation at your school.

SCHOOL MISSION AND VISION
(As you consider these questions you may want to refer to chapters 1 and 2.)

- Does our school have a clear philosophy and position statement around biblical worldview and spiritual formation? If so, how is it communicated?

- Does our school engage in culture-building conversations that lead to the implementation of improved systems and practices?

- In what ways do our mission and vision spark conversations in our school community that are grounded in biblical truth and driven by the knowledge of Christ and His purposes for life?

- Are our philosophy and practices aligned with our sponsoring church or the Church at large?

- Have we considered inculcating worldview development, biblical literacy, apologetics, ethics, spiritual disciplines, and spiritual formation into our overall school—wide objectives? If so, how are they evidenced?

- Within our mission and vision, how do we recognize the important role that both church and family play in the spiritual formation of students?

Action Steps that emerge from considering these questions:

SCHOOL LEADERSHIP:
(As you consider these questions you may want to refer to chapters 3, 6, and 8.)

- What scriptures have grounded our leadership team in their biblical worldview positions?

- In what ways has leadership prioritized spiritual formation and biblical worldview development in the school?

- How has our school leadership demonstrated a clear understanding of the value of biblical worldview and spiritual formation in its hiring and onboarding practices?

- Can our leaders articulate a clear plan for ongoing faculty and student development in the areas of biblical worldview and spiritual formation?

- Has our school leadership been challenged with personal spiritual formation goals? In what way?

- Can our leadership explicitly state the ways in which biblical worldview informs our decisions?

- How does our leadership keep staff accountable for the development of worldview, discipleship, and the spiritual formation of students?

- Does school leadership invite questions and encourage debate around difficult cultural issues? If so, how is this communicated to staff and students?

- In what ways has our leadership encouraged parent education and partnership in the area of biblical worldview development and spiritual formation?

- In what ways is our leadership proactively facing the challenges of increasing secularism and various other worldviews in the current culture?

- Has our school leadership implemented a faith development assessment instrument to determine whether the school is meeting its faith development objectives/outcomes?

Action Steps that emerge from considering these questions:

SCHOOL POLICY
(As you consider these questions you may want to refer to chapter 3.)

- Do our admissions and enrollment policies reflect the God-given value of all children, recognizing them as God's image bearers (*imago Dei*)?

- In what ways do we recognize in our policies that the spiritual formation of students is a lifelong journey, making room for forgiveness, grace, and reconciliation?

- How do our hiring policies and practices ensure that all staff members hold a biblical worldview and are deepening that worldview?

- In what ways do our policies create an accountability process for the ongoing spiritual formation of every employee?

- How can our policies ensure that every board member lives out a biblical worldview and is engaged in an ongoing process of spiritual formation?

- How do our policies reflect a biblical worldview around finances and stewardship?

Action Steps that emerge from considering these questions:

CURRICULUM DEVELOPMENT/ PEDAGOGY
(As you consider these questions you may want to refer to chapters 4, 5, 6, 7, and 8.)

- Do we see missing personnel needs in our school that, if in place, could help foster a clearer understanding of biblical integration in the curriculum?

- What training in biblical integration and spiritual formation may be needed for our faculty?

- Is there ongoing support for teachers as they refine their understanding of biblical integration and develop their techniques?

- Do we have a curriculum map that is regularly reviewed to ensure biblical worldview integration components in the curriculum?

- Have teachers in our school been given a framework from which they develop essential biblical worldview questions around their content?

- Does our pedagogical approach enable students to not only obtain biblical literacy, but also to apply that literacy both within the classroom and outside of the classroom?

- Are teachers within our school able to develop and pose a worldview essential question related to the content of a lesson and articulate a biblical answer?

- Do lesson plans demonstrate activities that allow students time to process content utilizing the essential worldview question in addition to providing the cultivation of faith in practice?

- In what ways do our curriculum and methods of classroom management point our students to the presence and authority of God?

- How do we create a culture in our classrooms where our students learn, watch, and participate in actions that will help them develop a natural desire to love God and love others, through the help and enabling of the Holy Spirt?

- How can we prioritize the needed time for teachers to engage with their curriculum in the creation of quality biblical integration and intentional spiritual formation activities?

- What new or redeployed resources are needed to help guide biblical integration in our curriculum development?

- What guidelines are provided to teachers that allow our students to flourish in their unique spiritual gifts, talents, and abilities within the classroom?

- How are teachers trained in areas of pedagogy that engage our students in thoughtful reflection, higher-order thinking, and questioning around their biblical worldview?

- What strategies are used to assist our students in understanding their place in God's story throughout the teaching and learning process?

- Do our classrooms intentionally and explicitly connect students to God's redemptive storyline?

Action Steps that emerge from considering these questions:

INTERNAL RELATIONSHIPS
(As you consider these questions you may want to refer to chapters 6 and 7.)

- How does our school emphasize the relational aspects of the school community (e.g., kindness, empathy, love, grace, generosity, forgiveness, etc.)?

- In what ways do we invite, nurture, and empower God's image-bearing teachers and students to join Him in His redemptive work of making all things new again, as they learn and grow together in relationship with one another?

- How do we foster a sense of belonging and community building for all the students attending our school?

- Do our teachers and school leaders have an appropriate amount of allocated time for communicating effectively and engaging with parents regarding the spiritual formation of their child and the importance of partnership?

- Is there an expectation of relationship building between our school staff and students? If so, what structures and accountability measures are in place?

- How are healthy peer-to-peer relationships between our faculty members fostered?

- Is leadership interdependence (recognition and utilization of unique giftings) demonstrated among the board and school leadership?

- How does our leadership demonstrate care and compassion for the staff and consider their work-life balance within both stated and unstated expectations?

Action Steps that emerge from considering these questions:

SOCIAL AND CULTURAL ENGAGEMENT
(As you consider these questions you may want to refer to chapters 7 and 9.)

- What processes are in place that prepare our staff members to care for the social and emotional wellbeing of our students from a biblical perspective?

- Are there systems in place to handle social/emotional crises within our school?

- Do we have curriculum in place for social/emotional learning from a biblical worldview?

- How do our teachers help to foster age-appropriate cultural engagement, creating an awareness of the world's brokenness and a sense of agency as Christ's ambassadors?

- In what ways has our school moved toward a service-learning model to equip students to become the hands and feet of Christ in our community?

- How do our teachers and leaders model Christian service and cultural engagement?

Action Steps that emerge from considering these questions:

EXTERNAL RELATIONSHIPS
(As you consider these questions you may want to refer to chapters 7 and 9.)

- How does our school demonstrate gratitude and care for our donors and external volunteers?

- In what way does our school intentionally minister to vendors, neighbors, first responders, and others who serve our school in the external community?

- How does our school pursue and practice ways to care for God's creation?

- How does learning extend beyond the classroom in our school?

- Is there a plan in our school to foster biblical unity and healing in the broken and divided areas of our community?

- Does our school community foster relationships and partnerships with local community groups, hospitals, etc. to extend the hands and feet of Christ? If so, how can that become more strategic in our school?

Action Steps that emerge from considering these questions:

CHRISTIAN EDUCATION ADVOCACY

Extending your creative thinking toward advocacy:

- To what degree have we built outreach programs to local churches and built relationships with pastors that lead them to a better understanding of the value of Christian education and the connection to their own goals of the spiritual formation of students and families?

- How have we engaged with local politicians in advocating for religious liberty issues that impact Christian education and the school's ability to effectively integrate biblical worldview in all areas of instruction and school life?

- Have we been strategic in helping prospective parents understand the purposes of Christian education and the impact of biblical worldview thinking and learning?
- Have we made the case for Christian education and biblical worldview thinking in our marketing materials and media guide?

Action Steps that emerge from considering these questions:

REFERENCES

Introduction

Barna Group. 2022. *The Open Generation: A Global Teens Study*. Ventura, CA: Author.

Hughes, Richard, and William B. Adrian (Eds.). 1997. *Models for Christian Higher Education: Strategies for Survival and Success in the Twenty-First Century*. Grand Rapids, MI: Wm. B. Eerdmans Publishing.

Graham, Donovan L. 2003. *Teaching Redemptively: Bringing Grace and Truth into Your Classroom*. Colorado Springs, CO: Purposeful Design Publishing.

Hull, John E. 2003. "Aiming for Christian Education, Settling for Christians Educating: The Christian School's Replication of a Public School Paradigm," *Christian Scholar's Review* 32 no. 2: 203–22.

Swaner, Lynn E. 2016. *Professional Development for Christian School Educators and Leaders: Frameworks and Best Practices*. Colorado Springs, CO: Association of Christian Schools International.

Swaner, Lynn E., and Andy Wolfe. 2021. *Flourishing Together: A Christian Vision for Students, Educators, and Schools*. Grand Rapids, MI: Wm. B. Eerdmans.

Part I: Philosophy and Research

1. Biblical Worldview and Spiritual Formation: Frameworks and Definitions

BibleProject. Biblical Literary Styles Bible Intro Video: Bibleproject™. Accessed January 5, 2023. https://bibleproject.com/explore/video/literary-styles-bible/.

Crabb, Larry. 1987. *Understanding People: Deep Longings for Relationship*. Grand Rapids, MI: Zondervan.

Geisler, Norman L., and Thomas A. Howe. 2004. *When Critics Ask: A Popular Handbook on Bible Difficulties*. Grand Rapids, MI: Baker Books.

Hoffecker, W. Andrew. 2007. *Revolutions in Worldview Understanding the Flow of Western Thought*. Phillipsburg, NJ: P&R Publishing.

Hoffecker, W. Andrew, and John D Currid. 2007. "The Hebrew World-and-Life View." In *Revolutions in Worldview: Understanding the Flow of Western Thought*. Phillipsburg, NJ: P&R Publishing.

Kuyper, Abraham. 2022. *Calvinism: The Stone Lectures*. Moscow, ID: Canon Press.

Moreland, James Porter, and William Lane Craig. 2017. *Philosophical Foundations for a Christian Worldview*. Downers Grove, IL: IVP Academic.

Nash, Ronald H. 2010. *Worldviews in Conflict: Choosing Christianity in a World of Ideas*. Grand Rapids, MI: Zondervan.

Naugle, David K. 2005. *Worldview: The History of a Concept*. Grand Rapids, MI: Wm. B. Eerdmans Publishing.

Plantinga, Cornelius. 2002. *Engaging God's World: A Christian Vision of Faith, Learning, and Living.* Grand Rapids, MI: Wm. B. Eerdmans Publishing.

Williamson, G. I. 2004. *The Westminster Confession of Faith for Study Classes.* Phillipsburg, NJ: P&R Publishing.

2. Biblical Worldview and Spiritual Formation: Insights from Research

Acree, Amanda Jeanette. 1994. "Instilling a Biblical Worldview by Addressing Postmodernity: Best Practices of Postsecondary Christian Faculty." Ed.D., Oral Roberts University.

Ali, Akhtar. 2014. "Comparing Religious Maturity of Hindu, Christian and Muslin Secondary School Students." *Muhammad Ayoub* no. 22 (4): 1–8.

Anderson, David W. 2003. "Special Education as Reconciliation." *Journal of Education and Christian Belief* no. 7 (2003): 22–36.

— 2011. "Hospitable Classrooms: Biblical Hospitality and Inclusive Education." *Journal of Education and Christian Belief* no. 15 (2011): 13–27.

Arold, Benjamin W., Ludger Woessmann, and Larissa Zierow. 2022. "Can Schools Change Religious Attitudes? Evidence from German State Reforms of Compulsory Religious Education." CESifo Working Paper No. 9504: Ludwigs-Maximilians University's Center for Economic Studies and the IFO Institute.

Astin, Alexander W., Helen S. Astin, Jennifer A. Lindholm, Alyssa N. Bryant, Shannon Calderone, and Katalin Szelényi. 2004. "The Spiritual Life of College Students: A National Study of College Students' Search for Meaning and Purpose." Higher Education Research Institute.

Baley, Steven Richard. 2021. "Developing a Biblical Worldview of Human Dignity in the High School Students of Twin Tiers Christian Academy in Breesport, New York." D.Ed.Min., Southern Baptist Theological Seminary.

Baniszewski, David E. 2016. "A Causal Comparative Analysis of Biblical Worldview among Graduate Students Based on Christian School Attendance." Ed.D.: Liberty University.

Banke, Susan, Nancy Maldonado, and Candace H. Lacey. 2012. "Christian School Leaders and Spirituality." *Journal of Research on Christian Education* no. 21 (3): 235–264.

Barke, Steven Jonathan Jacob. 2014. "Conveying a Biblical Worldview to Charter School Students: A Pilot Study." D.Min., Talbot School of Theology.

Barna Group. 2007. "A New Generation Expresses Its Skepticism and Frustration with Christianity." Barna Group. https://www.barna.com/research/a-new-generation-expresses-its-skepticism-and-frustration-with-christianity/ September 21, 2007.

Barna Group, and ACSI. 2017. "Multiple Choice: How Parents Sort Education Options in a Changing Market." Colorado Springs, CO: Association of Christian Schools International.

References

Barrows, Donald Kevin. 2014. "Understanding the Times: A Causal/Comparative Study of the Effectiveness of a Christian Worldview Curriculum in Helping Students Develop a Christian Worldview." Ed.D., Liberty University.

Bartkowski, John P., Xiaohe Xu, and Martin L. Levin. 2008. "Religion and Child Development: Evidence from the Early Childhood Longitudinal Study." *Social Science Research* no. 37 (1): 18–36.

Beckman, Jack E., James L. Drexler, and Kevin J. Eames. 2012. " 'Faithful Presence': The Christian School Head, Personhood, Relationships, and Outcomes." *Journal of School Choice* no. 6 (1): 104–27.

Benson, P. L., M. J. Donahue, and J. A. Erickson. 1993. "The Faith Maturity Scale: Conceptualization, Measurement and Empirical Validation." *Research in the Social Scientific Study of Religion* no. 5: 1–26.

Blos, Peter. 1967. "The Second Individuation Process of Adolescence." *The Psychoanalytic Study of the Child* no. 22 (1): 162–86.

Boyatzis, Chris J., and Denise L. Janicki. 2003. "Parent-Child Communication about Religion: Survey and Diary Data on Unilateral Transmission and Bi-Directional Reciprocity Styles." *Review of Religious Research* no. 44 (3): 252–70.

Braskamp, Larry A. 2007. "Fostering Religious and Spiritual Development of Students during College." Brooklyn, NY: Social Science Research Council.

Brickhill, Cherie Elder. 2010. "A Comparative Analysis of Factors Influencing the Development of a Biblical Worldview in Christian Middle-School Students." Ed.D., Lynchburg, VA: Liberty University.

Brinkley, Thomas David. 2021. "Teaching Christian Worldview at Rosslyn Academy: An Assessment and Strategy for Worldview Instruction in an International School Setting." D.Min., Southeastern Baptist Theological Seminary.

Bryant, Michael Hugh. 2008. "A Comparative Analysis of Factors Contributing to the Biblical Worldview among High School Students in the American Association of Christian Schools of Georgia, North Carolina, and South Carolina." Ed.D.: Liberty University.

Burch, Michael J., Patricia Swails, and Randy Mills. 2015. "Perceptions of Administrators' Servant Leadership Qualities at a Christian University: A Descriptive Study." *Education* no. 135 (4): 399–404.

Cardus. 2019a. "Cardus Education Survey 2018: Perceptions of High School Experience and Preparedness for Life." Hamilton, ON: Cardus.

— 2019b. "Cardus Education Survey 2018: Involved and Engaged." Hamilton, ON: Cardus.

— 2019c. "Cardus Education Survey 2018: Spiritual Strength, Faithful Formation." Hamilton, ON: Cardus.

Casagrande, Maria, Ray Pennings, and David Sikkink. 2019. "Cardus Education Survey 2018: Rethinking Public Education." Hamilton, ON: Cardus.

Chen, Ying, Christina Hinton, and Tyler J. VanderWeele. 2021. "School Types in Adolescence and Subsequent Health and Well-Being in Young Adulthood: An Outcome-Wide Analysis." *PLOS ONE* no. 16 (11): e0258723.

Cheng, Albert. 2018. "The Educational Emphases of Science Teachers in US Evangelical Protestant High Schools." SSRN Scholarly Paper ID 3193028. Rochester, NY: Social Science Research Network.

Cheng, Albert, Rian Djita, and David Hunt. 2022. "Many Educational Systems, a Common Good." Hamilton, ON: Cardus.

Cheng, Albert, and Darren Iselin. 2020. "The Cardus Education Survey Australia: Australian Schools and the Common Good." Hamilton, ON: Cardus.

Cheng, Albert, Matthew H. Lee, and Rian Djita. 2022. "A Cross-Sectional Analysis of the Relationship Between Sabbath Practices and US, Canadian, Indonesian, and Paraguayan Teachers' Burnout." *Journal of Religion and Health*, September.

Cheng, Albert, and David Sikkink. 2020. "A Longitudinal Analysis of Volunteerism Activities for Individuals Educated in Public and Private Schools." *Youth & Society* no. 52 (7): 1193–1219.

Cheng, Albert, Patrick J. Wolf, Wendy Wang, and W. Bradford Wilcox. 2020. "The Protestant Family Ethic: What Do Protestant, Catholic, Private, and Public Schooling Have to Do with Marriage, Divorce, and Non-Marital Childbearing?" Washington, DC: American Enterprise Institute and the Institute for Family Studies.

Cookson, Gary, and Samuel J. Smith. 2011. "Establishing Special Education Programs: Experiences of Christian School Principals." *Journal of Research on Christian Education* no. 20 (3): 239–53.

Cooling, Trevor. 2005. "Curiosity: Vice or Virtue for the Christian Teacher? Promoting Faithfulness to scripture in Teacher Formation." *Journal of Education and Christian Belief* no. 9 (2): 87–103.

Cort, Alec Kyle. 2008. "The Relationship of Adolescent Perceptions of Peer Acceptance and Motivation to Participate in the Local Congregation." Ed.D.: Southern Baptist Theological Seminary.

Cunningham, Bryan. 2012. *Mentoring Teachers in Post-Compulsory Education.* Routledge.

Deckard, Steve, Tom Henderson, and Darren Grant. 2002. "The Importance of the Teacher's Worldview in Relationship to Student Understanding of the Creation and Evolution Controversy." *Christian Education Journal* no. 6 (2).

Deckard, Steve, and Gregory M. Sobko. 1998. "Toward the Development of an Instrument for Measuring a Christian Creationist Worldview." *Proceedings of the International Conference on Creationism* no. 4.

DeHaan, Robert, Russell Hanford, Kathleen Kinlaw, David Philler, and John Snarey. 1997. "Promoting Ethical Reasonings Affect and Behaviour Among High School Students: An Evaluation of Three Teaching Strategies." *Journal of Moral Education* no. 26 (1): 5–20.

Drexler, James, and Amy H. Bagby. 2021. "Defining and Assessing Spiritual Formation: A Necessity for Christian Schooling." *International Christian Community of Teacher Educators Journal* no. 16 (1).

Drexler, James L., ed. 2007. *Schools as Communities: Educational Leadership, Relationships, and the Eternal Value of Christian Schooling*. Colorado Springs, CO: Purposeful Design Publications.

Erickson, Joseph A. 1992. "Adolescent Religious Development and Commitment: A Structural Equation Model of the Role of Family, Peer Group, and Educational Influences." *Journal for the Scientific Study of Religion* no. 31 (2): 131.

Evans, Mitchell Grady. 2015. "An Analysis of the Biblical Worldview of High School Educators in ACSI Schools." Ed.D.: Southeastern Baptist Theologial Seminary.

Family Research Council. 2017. "Hostility to Religion: The Growing Threat to Religious Liberty in the United States." Washington, DC: Family Research Council.

Fawcett, Bruce G., Leslie J. Francis, and Ursula McKenna. 2021. "Sustaining Young Canadian Baptists in the Faith: Exploring the Connection between Religious Affect and Parental Religious Attendance." *Journal of Research on Christian Education* no. 30 (3): 317–36.

— 2022. "The Connection between Teenage Religious Affect and Parental Church Attendance: A Study among Young Canadian Baptists." *Research in Brief* 4 (1): 6–11.

Fowler, James W. 1995. *Stages of Faith: The Psychology of Human Development and the Quest for Meaning*. New York, NY: Harper One.

Fullerton, J. Timothy, and Bruce Hunsberger. 1982. "A Unidimensional Measure of Christian Orthodoxy." *Journal for the Scientific Study of Religion* no. 21 (4): 317.

Fyock, James A. 2008. "The Effect of the Teacher's Worldviews on the Worldviews of High School Seniors." Ed.D., Liberty University.

Gantt, Susan Denise. 2004. "Catechetical Instruction as an Educational Process for the Teaching of Doctrine to Children in Southern Baptist Churches." Ph.D., Southern Baptist Theological Seminary.

Garber, Steven. 2007. *The Fabric of Faithfulness: Weaving Together Belief and Behavior*. Expanded ed. Downers Grove, IL: IVP.

Gottfried, Michael, and Jacob Kirksey. 2018. "Self-Discipline and Catholic Education: Evidence from Two National Cohorts." Washington, DC: Thomas B. Fordham Institute.

Graham, Donovan L. 2003. *Teaching Redemptively: Bringing Grace and Truth into Your Classroom*. Colorado Springs, CO: Purposeful Design Publications.

Green, Beth, Doug Sikkema, David Sikkink, Sara Skiles, and Ray Pennings. 2016. "Cardus Education Survey 2016: Educating to Love Your Neighbour." Hamilton, ON: Cardus.

Gunnoe, Marjorie Lindner, and Kristin A. Moore. 2002. "Predictors of Religiosity Among Youth Aged 17–22: A Longitudinal Study of the National Survey of Children." *Journal for the Scientific Study of Religion* no. 41 (4): 613–22.

Hardy, Sam A., Jenae M. Nelson, Joseph P. Moore, and Pamela Ebstyne King. 2019. "Processes of Religious and Spiritual Influence in Adolescence: A Systematic Review of 30 Years of Research." *Journal of Research on Adolescence* no. 29 (2): 254–75.

Harrison, Brandy. 2018. "Christian Ed Grads." *Christian Courier* (blog). March 26, 2018. http://www.christiancourier.ca/news/entry/christian-ed-grads.

Harrison, Suzanne. 2012. "Leadership in Private Christian Schools: Perceptions of Administrators." *International Christian Community of Teacher Educators Journal* no. 8 (1): 1–14.

Haynes, Michael B. 2006. "The Integration of Church and Home: A Strategic Partnership for Spiritual Formation." D.Min.: Liberty University.

Hembree, John R. 2007. "Biblical Worldview Integration for Effective Ministry." D.Min., Assemblies of God Theological Seminary.

Henderson, Tom, Steve Deckard, and David A. DeWitt. 2003. "Impact of a Young-Earth Creationist Apologetics Course on Student Creation Worldview." *Journal of Creation* no. 17: 111–16.

Hill, Jonathan P. 2009. "Higher Education as Moral Community: Institutional Influences on Religious Participation During College." *Journal for the Scientific Study of Religion* no. 48 (3): 515–34.

Hill, Peter C., and Ralph W. Hood, eds. 1999. *Measures of Religiosity*. Birmingham, AL: Religious Education Press.

Hitlin, Steven, and Jane Allyn Piliavin. 2004. "Values: Reviving a Dormant Concept." *Annual Review of Sociology* no. 30 (1): 359–93.

Holder, Mark D., Ben Coleman, Tim Krupa, and Eugene Krupa. 2016. "Well-Being's Relation to Religiosity and Spirituality in Children and Adolescents in Zambia." *Journal of Happiness Studies* no. 17 (3): 1235–53.

Holloway, Derek, Anne Lumb, Liz Mills, Andrew Rickett, Shahne Vickery, Tatiana Wilson, and Kathryn Wright. 2019. "Spiritual Development: Interpretations of Spiritual Development in the Classroom." London, UK: The National Society for the Promotion of Education.

Huber, Stefan, and Odilo W. Huber. 2012. "The Centrality of Religiosity Scale (CRS)." *Religions* no. 3 (3): 710–24.

Hunsberger, Bruce. 1989. "A Short Version of the Christian Orthodoxy Scale." *Journal for the Scientific Study of Religion* no. 28 (3): 360.

Hunter, James Davison. 2008. *Death of Character: Moral Education in an Age Without Good or Evil*. New York: Basic Books.

Iannaccone, Laurence R. 1990. "Religious Practice: A Human Capital Approach." *Journal for the Scientific Study of Religion* no. 29 (3): 297–314.

Iselin, Darren, and John D. Meteyard. 2010. "The 'Beyond in the Midst': An Incarnational Response to the Dynamic Dance of Christian Worldview, Faith and Learning." *Journal of Education and Christian Belief* no. 14 (1): 33–46.

References

Kanitz, Lori. 2005. "Improving Christian Worldview Pedagogy: Going Beyond Mere Christianity." *Christian Higher Education* no. 4 (2): 99–108.

Kimball, Miles, Colter Mitchell, Arland Thornton, and Linda Young-Demarco. 2009. "Empirics on the Origins of Preferences: The Case of College Major and Religiosity." Cambridge, MA: National Bureau of Economic Research.

Kim-Spoon, Jungmeen, Gregory S. Longo, and Michael E. McCullough. 2012. "Parent-Adolescent Relationship Quality as a Moderator for the Influences of Parents' Religiousness on Adolescents' Religiousness and Adjustment." *Journal of Youth and Adolescence* no. 41 (12): 1576–87.

King, Pamela Ebstyne, James L. Furrow, and Natalie Roth. 2002. "The Influence of Families and Peers on Adolescent Religiousness." *Journal of Psychology and Christianity* no. 21 (2): 109–20.

Kovacs, Eszter, Bettina Franciska Piko, and Kevin Michael Fitzpatrick. 2011. "Religiosity as a Protective Factor Against Substance Use Among Hungarian High School Students." *Substance Use & Misuse* 46 (10): 1346–57.

Krause, Neal, and Christopher G. Ellison. 2007. "Parental Religious Socialization Practices and Self-Esteem in Late Life." *Review of Religious Research* no. 49 (2): 109–27.

Krispin, Keith Richard. 2004. "The Relationship between Youth Ministry Involvement and Faith Maturity in First-Year Students in a Christian College." Ed.D., Southern Baptist Theological Seminary.

Kroger, Jane. 2003. "Identity Development during Adolescence." In *Blackwell Handbook of Adolescence*, edited by Gerald R. Adams and Michael D. Berzonsky, 205–26. Malden, MA: Blackwell Publishing.

Krok, Dariusz. 2018. "Examining the Role of Religion in a Family Setting: Religious Attitudes and Quality of Life among Parents and Their Adolescent Children." *Journal of Family Studies* no. 24 (3): 203–18.

Lee, Jerry W., Gail T. Rice, and V. Bailey Gillespie. 1997. "Family Worship Patterns and Their Correlation with Adolescent Behavior and Beliefs." *Journal for the Scientific Study of Religion* no. 36 (3): 372–81.

Lee, Matthew H. 2021. "Faith-Based Education and Civic Value Formation." Ph.D., University of Arkansas.

Lee, Matthew H., and Albert Cheng. 2021. "The Preparation and Practice of Protestant School Leadership: Evidence from a Nationally Representative U.S. Sample." *Journal of Research on Christian Education*, October, 1–26.

Lee, Matthew H., Albert Cheng, and Kathryn Wiens. 2021. "2020 Principal Survey." Kennesaw, GA: Council on Educational Standards & Accountability.

Lee, Matthew H., and Eric W. Price. 2022. "ACSI Schools Weather Pandemic Storm with Steady Student Achievement, in-Person Instruction, and Enrollment Growth." Colorado Springs, CO: Association of Christian Schools International. https://www.acsi.org/docs/default-source/website-publishing/research/acsi-schools-weather-pandemic-storm.pdf.

Lee, Matthew H., Eric W. Price, and Lynn E. Swaner. 2022. "The Effect of Private School Choice Regulations on School Participation: Experimental Evidence from the Christian School Sector." *Journal of School Choice*, August, 1–19.

Leonard, Kathleen C., Kaye V. Cook, Chris J. Boyatzis, Cynthia Neal Kimball, and Kelly S. Flanagan. 2013. "Parent-Child Dynamics and Emerging Adult Religiosity: Attachment, Parental Beliefs, and Faith Support." *Psychology of Religion and Spirituality* no. 5 (1): 5–14.

Long, Thomas J., and Merylann J. Schuttloffel. 2006. "A Rationale for Special Education in Catholic Schools." *Catholic Education: A Journal of Inquiry and Practice* no. 9 (4): 443–52.

Lovik, Eric G. 2010. "The Impact of Organizational Features and Student Experiences on Spiritual Development during the First Year of College." Ph.D., Pennyslvania State University.

MacIntyre, Alasdair C. 2007. *After Virtue: A Study in Moral Theory*. 3rd ed. Notre Dame, IN: University of Notre Dame Press.

Marks, Loren. 2004. "Sacred Practices in Highly Religious Families: Christian, Jewish, Mormon, and Muslim Perspectives." *Family Process* no. 43 (2): 217–31.

Martin, Todd F., James M. White, and Daniel Perlman. 2003. "Religious Socialization: A Test of the Channeling Hypothesis of Parental Influence on Adolescent Faith Maturity." *Journal of Adolescent Research* no. 18 (2): 169–87.

Mercer, David. 2015. "Educating Students with Disabilities in Regional Independent Christian Schools of Queensland." *Journal of the Christian Institute on Disability* 4 (2).

Meyer, Raymond Keith. 2003. "A Comparative Analysis of the Factors Contributing to the Biblical Worldview of Students Enrolled in a Christian School." Ed.D., Southern Baptist Theological Seminary.

Mills, Kathy A. 2003. "The Culture of the Christian School." *Journal of Education and Christian Belief* no. 7 (2): 129–42.

Mooney, Tanya R. 2018. "A Case Study of Professional Development Activities That Foster a Biblical Worldview in K–8 Christian School Teachers." Ed.D., Lynchburg, VA: Liberty University.

Murray, Robert J. 2011. "Hiring School Counselors in Faith-Based Schools." *Journal of Catholic Education* no. 15 (1).

Olwyn, Mark. 2016. *Passing on Faith*. London, UK: Theos.

Oosterhuis, Alyce. 2002. "The Development of a Christian Ideology of Inclusive Education." *Journal of Research on Christian Education* no. 11 (1): 5–31.

Pakaluk, Catherine Ruth. 2021. "What Good Is a Good Fit? Religious Matching and Educational Outcomes." *Cosmos + Taxis* no. 9 (1–2): 3–30.

Pennings, Ray, David Sikkink, and Ashley Berner. 2014. "Private Schools for the Public Good." Hamilton, ON: Cardus.

Pennings, Ray, and Kathryn Wiens. 2011. "Do the Motivations for Private Religious Catholic and Protestant Schooling in North America Align with Graduate Outcomes?" Hamilton, ON: Cardus.

Perkins, Jennifer Lea. 2007. "Differences in Biblical Worldview Scores of Southern Baptist Adolescents across Variables of Family Functioning and Family Discipleship." Ph.D., Southern Baptist Theological Seminary.

Peterson, Bill E. 2006. "Generativity and Successful Parenting: An Analysis of Young Adult Outcomes." *Journal of Personality* no. 74 (3): 847–70.

Peterson, Daniel Carl. 2012. "A Comparative Analysis of the Integration of Faith and Learning between ACSI and ACCS Accredited Schools." Ph.D., Southern Baptist Theological Seminary.

Petts, R. J. 2011. "Parental Religiosity, Religious Homogamy, and Young Children's Well-Being." *Sociology of Religion* no. 72 (4): 389–414.

Pew Research Center. 2015. "America's Changing Religious Landscape: Christians Decline Sharply as Share of Population; Unaffiliated and Other Faiths Continue to Grow." Washington, DC: Pew Research Center.

Plantinga, Alvin. 2015. *Knowledge and Christian Belief.* Grand Rapids, MI: William B. Eerdmans Publishing.

Ray, Donald David. 2001. "The Relationship of High School Students' Attitudes towards Creation and Evolution with the Students' Worldview Philosophy." Ed.D., Southern Baptist Theological Seminary.

Regnerus, Mark D., Christian Smith, and Brad Smith. 2004. "Social Context in the Development of Adolescent Religiosity." *Applied Developmental Science* no. 8 (1): 27–38.

Rixford, Mary Ewing. 1997. "From the Walls of the City: Disabilities as Culture." *Journal of Pastoral Care* no. 51 (2): 151–64.

Russo, Charles J. 2009. "The Law and Hiring Practices in Faith-Based Schools." *Journal of Research on Christian Education* no. 18 (3): 256–71.

Rutledge, David S. 2013. "An Analysis of the Correlation between the Christian Education Context of the Local Church and the Biblical Worldview of High School Students." Ed.D., Liberty University.

Saphier, Jon, and Matthew King. 1985. "Good Seeds Grow in Strong Cultures." *Educational Leadership* no. 42 (6): 67–74.

Schultz, Katherine G. 2012. "Developing an Instrument for Assessing Student Biblical Worldview." Ed.D., Regent University.

Schwartz, Kelly Dean. 2006. "RESEARCH: Transformations in Parent and Friend Faith Support Predicting Adolescents' Religious Faith." *International Journal for the Psychology of Religion* no. 16 (4): 311–26.

Schwarz, Jonathan, and David Sikkink. 2017. "Promises, Promises." Hamilton, ON: Cardus.

Sikkink, David. 2012. "Religious School Differences in School Climate and Academic Mission: A Descriptive Overview of School Organization and Student Outcomes." *Journal of School Choice* 6 (1): 20–39.

— 2018a. "Bringing Thou Back In." Hamilton, ON: Cardus.

— 2018b. "Walking the Path: The Religious Lives of Young Adults in North America." Hamilton, ON: Cardus.

Simoneaux, Carolyn Potts. 2015. "A Comparative Analysis of Worldview Development and Religious Commitment between Apostolic College Students Attending Apostolic Christian and Secular Colleges." Ed.D., Liberty University.

Smith, Christian. 2009. *Soul Searching: The Religious and Spiritual Lives of American Teenagers*. Oxford, England: Oxford University Press.

Smith, David. 2009. *On Christian Teaching: Practicing Faith in the Classroom*. Grand Rapids, MI: Wm. B. Eerdmans Publishing.

Smith, David I., Beth Green, Mia Kurkechian, and Albert Cheng. 2021. "Assessing Christian Learning: Towards a Practices-Based Approach to Faith, Vocation, and Assessment." *International Journal of Christianity & Education* no. 25 (2): 151–68.

Smith, David, and James K. A. Smith, eds. 2011. *Teaching and Christian Practices: Reshaping Faith and Learning*. Grand Rapids, MI: Wm. B. Eerdmans Publishing.

Spears, Wayne D. 2005. "Discovering the Catalysts for Growing True Disciples in an Emerging Postmodern Culture." D.Min., Asbury Theological Seminary.

Swaner, Lynn E., Cindy Dodds, and Matthew H. Lee. 2021. *Leadership for Flourishing Schools: From Research to Practice*. Colorado Springs, CO: Association of Christian Schools International.

Swaner, Lynn E., Charlotte A. Marshall, and Sheri A. Tesar. 2019. *Flourishing Schools: Research on Christian School Culture and Community*. Colorado Springs, CO: Association of Christian Schools International.

Taylor, Larry A. 2009. "A Study of the Biblical Worldview of Twelfth Grade Students from Christian and Public High School." Ph.D., Dallas Baptist University.

Uecker, Jeremy E. 2008. "Alternative Schooling Strategies and the Religious Lives of American Adolescents." *Journal for the Scientific Study of Religion* no. 47 (4): 563–84.

Van Meter, Kenneth G. 2009. "The Order of Importance of Component Parts of the Biblical Worldview in Christian High School Students." Ed.D., George Fox University.

Volkwein, J. Fredericks. 2010. "A Model for Assessing Institutional Effectiveness." *New Directions for Institutional Research*. S1: 13–28.

Walton, Julie A. P., and Matthew Walters. 2011. "Eat This Class: Breaking Bread in the Undergraduate Classroom." In *Teaching and Christian Practices: Reshaping Faith and Learning*, edited by David Smith and James K. A. Smith, 80–101. Grand Rapids, MI: Wm. B. Eerdmans Publishing.

White, Fiona A., and Kenan M. Matawie. 2004. "Parental Morality and Family Processes as Predictors of Adolescent Morality." *Journal of Child and Family Studies* no. 13 (2): 219–33.

Willard, Dallas. 2002. *Renovation of the Heart: Putting on the Character of Christ.* Colorado Springs, CO: NavPress.

Williams, Clayton R. 2021. "The Impact of Faith-Integration Training Programs on Teacher Self-Efficacy and Teaching from a Biblical Worldview." Ed.D., Union University.

Willits, Fern K., and Donald M. Crider. 1989. "Church Attendance and Traditional Religious Beliefs in Adolescence and Young Adulthood: A Panel Study." *Review of Religious Research* no. 31 (1): 68–81.

Wink, Paul, and Michele Dillon. 2002. "Parental Morality and Family Processes as Predictors of Adolescent Morality." *Journal of Adult Development* no. 9 (1): 79–94.

Wolf, Patrick J. 2007. "Civics Exam: Schools of Choice Boost Civic Values." *Education Next* no. 7 (3): 67–72.

Wolf, Patrick J., Albert Cheng, Wendy Wang, and W. Bradford Wilcox. 2022. "The School to Family Pipeline: What Do Religious, Private, and Public Schooling Have to Do with Family Formation?" *Journal of Catholic Education* no. 25 (1): 206–33.

Wood, Mark Kelly. 2008. "A Study of the Biblical Worldview of K–12 Christian School Educators." Ed.D., Liberty University.

Wynne, Edward A., and Herbert J. Walberg. 1985. "The Complementary Goals of Character Development and Academic Excellence." *Educational Leadership*, 15–18.

Yust, Karen-Marie. 2004. *Real Kids, Real Faith: Practices for Nurturing Children's Spiritual Lives.* San Francisco, CA: Jossey-Bass.

Part II: Christian School Perspectives

3. The Leadership Perspective: Christian Education's Distinctives

Gushee, David P. and Glen H. Stassen. 2016. *Kingdom Ethics: Following Jesus in Contemporary Context*, 2nd ed. Grand Rapids, MI: Wm. B. Eerdmans Publishing.

Naugle, David K. 2005. *Worldview: The History of a Concept.* Grand Rapids, MI: Wm. B. Eerdmans, Publishing. 2005.

Sire, James W. 2020. *The Universe Next Door: A Basic Worldview Catalog,* 6th ed. Westmont, IL: IVP Academic.

Taylor, Larry. 2013. *Running with the Horses: A Parenting Guide for Raising Children to Be Servant Leaders for Christ.* Bloomington, IN: WestBow Press.

4. The Teacher Perspective: Purposeful Cultivation

Anthony, Michael J., and Warren S. Benson. 2003. *History & Philosophy of Christian Education.* Eugene, OR: Wipf & Stock.

Augustine. 1995. *The Words of St. Augustine: Part III - Sermons.* Hyde Park, NY: New City Press.

Brooks, Christopher W. 2014. *Urban Apologetics.* Grand Rapids, MI: Kregel Publications.

Crouch, Andy. 2008. *Culture Making: Recovering Our Creative Calling.* Downers Grove, IL: IVP.

Guinness, Os. 2003. *The Call: Finding and Fulfilling the Central Purpose of Your Life.* Nashville, TN: Thomas Nelson.

Hoffecker, W. Andrew. 2007. *Revolutions in Worldview: Understanding the Flow of Western Thought.* Phillipsburg, NJ: P&R Publishing.

Neder, Adam. 2019. *Theology as a Way of Life: On Teaching and Learning the Christian Faith.* Grand Rapids, MI: Baker Academic.

Lewis, C.S. 1970. *Christian Apologetics.* Grand Rapids, MI: Wm. B. Eerdmans Publishing.

Pratt, Jr, Richard L. 2022. "The Value of Human Life." Tabletalk. January 21. Accessed January 21, 2022. https://tabletalkmagazine.com/posts/the-value-of-human-life/.

Prior, Karen Swallow. 2018. *On Reading Well: Finding the Good Life through Great Books.* Grand Rapids, MI: Brazos Press.

Propaganda, Sara Groves, Robbie Seay, and Audrey Assad. 2019. *Behold.*

Smith, David I., and James K. A. Smith. 2011. *Teaching and Christian Practices: Reshaping Faith & Learning.* Grand Rapids, MI: Wm. B. Eerdmans Publishing.

Smith, James K. A. 2016. *You Are What You Love: The Spiritual Power of Habit.* Grand Rapids, MI: Brazos Press.

Stonestreet, John, and Brett Kunkle. 2017. A *Practical Guide to Culture: Helping the Next Generation Navigate Today's World.* Colorado Springs, CO: David C Cook.

2020. The Westminster Shorter Catechism. Accessed December 7, 2022. https://www.westminsterconfession.org/resources/confessional-standards/the-westminster-shorter-catechism/.

Wenham, Gordon J. 2000. *Story as Torah: Reading the Old Testament Narrative Ethically.* Grand Rapids, MI: Baker Academic.

5. The Curricular Perspective: Biblical Worldview Integration

Beane, James A. 1995. *Toward a Coherent Curriculum.* Alexandria, VA: Association for Supervision and Curriculum Development.

Benson, D; Iselin, D., Messmore, R., and Murison C. 2017. *Locating Learning in God's Big Story 2.0: Illuminating Education in Australian Christian Schools.* Christian Schools Australia, New South Wales, Australia.

Jacobs, Heidi Hayes. 1997. *Mapping the Big Picture: Integrating Curriculum & Assessment K–12.* Alexandria, VA: Association for Supervision and Curriculum Development.

— 2004. *Getting Results with Curriculum Mapping.* Alexandria, VA: Association for Supervision and Curriculum Development.

MacCullough, Martha E. 2016. *Undivided: Developing a Worldview Approach to Biblical Integration.* Colorado Springs, CO: Purposeful Design Publications.

McTighe, Jay, and Grant P. Wiggins. 2013. *Essential Questions: Opening Doors to Student Understanding*. Alexandria, VA: Association for Supervision and Curriculum Development.

Richards, Larry, and Gary J. Bredfeldt. 2020. *Creative Bible Teaching*. Chicago, IL: Moody Publishers.

Sire, James W. 2020. *The Universe Next Door: A Basic Worldview Catalog*, 6th ed. Westmont, IL: IVP Academic.

6. The Faculty Development Perspective: Training Teachers for Biblical Worldview and Spiritual Formation

Cosgrove, Mark P. 2006. *Foundations of Christian Thought: Faith, Learning, and the Christian Worldview*. Grand Rapids, MI; Kregel Publications.

Fowler, James W. 1981. *Stages of Faith: The Psychology of Human Development and the Quest for Meaning*. San Francisco, CA: Harper & Row Publishers.

Guskey, Thomas R. 2002. *Evaluating Professional Development*. Thousand Oaks, CA: Corwin Press.

Hollinger, Dennis P. 2005. *Head, Heart, and Hands: Bringing Together Christian Thought, Passion, and Action*. Downers Grove, IL: IVP.

Joyce, Bruce, and Beverly Showers. 1982. "The Coaching of Teaching." *Educational Leadership* 40(1): 4–10.

— 2002. *Student Achievement Through Staff Development*, 3rd ed. Alexandria, VA: Associational for Supervision and Curriculum Development.

Knight, Jim. 2013. *Instructional Coaching: A Partnership Approach to Improving Instruction*. Thousand Oaks, CA: Corwin Press.

Noebel, David A., and Jeff Meyers. 2015. *Understanding the Times*. Manitou Springs, CO: Summit Ministries, 10.

Scott, Daniel G., and Douglas Magnuson. 2006. *Integrating Spiritual Development into Child and Youth Care Programs and Institutions*. Thousand Oaks, CA: SAGE Publications, Inc.

Smith, James K.A. 2016. *You Are What You Love: The Spiritual Power of Habit*. Grand Rapids, MI: Brazos Press.

Swaner, Lynn E. 2016. *Professional Development for Christian School Educators and Leaders: Frameworks and Best Practices*. Colorado Springs, CO: Association of Christian Schools International. Available at https://www.acsi.org/pdswaner.

Taylor, Larry. 2018. "Presentation of a Comprehensive Plan." Lecture at Kingdom School Institute, Plano, TX.

Teo, Wilson. 2017. "Christian Spiritual Formation." *Emerging Leadership Journeys* no. 10 (1): 138–150.

Willard, Dallas. 2002. *Renovation of the Heart: Putting on the Character of Christ*. Colorado Springs, CO: NavPress.

Part III: Programs and Practices

7. Teaching for Transformation (TfT): A Holistic Framework for Learning and Formation

Smith, James K.A. 2009. *Desiring the Kingdom: Worship, Worldview and Cultural Formation.* Grand Rapids, MI: Baker Academic.

— 2013. *Imagining the Kingdom: How Worship Works.* Grand Rapids, MI: Baker Academic.

8. At the Intersection of Faith and Learning: The Harkness Approach

Justin Smith, "The Harkness Approach Brings Student-Centered, Discussion-Based Learning to LRCA." *The Warrior*, Winter 2018, 10–12.

2020. The Westminster Shorter Catechism. Accessed December 7, 2022. https://www.westminsterconfession.org/resources/confessional-standards/the-westminster-shorter-catechism/.

9. Bringing Worldview and Formation "to Life": Service-Learning in Christian Schools

Astin, A. W., L. J. Sax, and J. Avalos. 1999. "Long-term Effects of Volunteerism During the Undergraduate Years." *Review of Higher Education* no. 2: 187–202.

Berson, J. S., and W. F. Younkin. 1998. "Doing well by doing good: A study of the effects of a service-learning experience on student success." Paper presented at the American Society of Higher Education, Miami, FL.

Erdvig, R.C.S. 2020. *Beyond Biblical Integration: Immersing You and Your Students in a Biblical Worldview.* Manitou Springs, CO: Summit Ministries.

Eyler, J., and D. E. Giles, Jr. 1999. *Where's the Learning in Service-Learning?* San Francisco: Jossey-Bass.

Felten, P., and P. Clayton. 2011. "Service-Learning." *New Directions for Teaching and Learning* no. 128:75–84.

Furco, A., and S. Root. 2010. "Research Demonstrates the Value of Service Learning." *Phi Delta Kappan* no. 5: 16–20.

Garber, S. 2014. *Visions of Vocation: Common Grace for the Common Good.* Westmont, IL: IVP.

Graham, D. 2009. *Teaching Redemptively: Bringing Grace and Truth into Your Classroom.* Colorado Springs, CO: Purposeful Design Publications.

Jacoby, Barbara and Assoc. 1996. *Service-Learning in Higher Education: Concepts and Practices.* San Francisco, CA Jossey-Bass.

Kaye, C. 2004. *The Complete Guide to Service-Learning.* Minneapolis, MN: Free Spirit Publishing.

Prentice, M. 2007. "Service-Learning and Civic Engagement." *Academic Questions* 20 no. 2: 135–145.

Radecke, M. W. 2007. "Service-Learning and Faith Formation." *Journal of College and Character* 8 no. 5: 1–28.

Smith, J. K. A. 2009. *Desiring the Kingdom: Worship, Worldview, and Cultural Formation.* Grand Rapids, MI: Baker Academic.

Stanton, T. K., D. E. Giles Jr., and N. I. Cruz. 1999. *Service-Learning: A Movement's Pioneers Reflect on Its Origins, Practice, and Future.* San Francisco, CA: Jossey-Bass.

Swaner, LE., and R.C.S. Erdvig. 2018. *Bring It to Life: Christian Education and the Transformative Power of Service-Learning.* Colorado Springs, CO: Purposeful Design Publications.

Vogelgesang, L. J., and A. W. Astin. 2000. "Comparing the Effects of Community Service and Service-Learning." *Michigan Journal of Community Service Learning* no. 7: 25–34.

Warren, J. 2012. "Does Service-Learning Increase Student Learning? A Meta-Analysis." *Michigan Journal of Community Service Learning* 18 no. 2: 56–61.

ABOUT THE AUTHORS

Darryl DeBoer has been involved in Christian education as a science teacher, outdoor education leader, and administrator in Canada, Switzerland, and India since 1996. Currently, he is the Director of Learning at Surrey Christian School (British Columbia), a Senior Fellow for the Center for the Advancement of Christian Education (CACE) at Dordt University, and the co-creator and Director of Teaching for Transformation (TfT). Darryl is most passionate about equipping teachers to design "real work, real needs, real people" learning experiences that invite, nurture, and empower themselves and their students to play their part within God's story.

Cindy Dodds has been in Christian school leadership for over twenty years. During that time, she led two formative-level schools from a deficit budget to a place of financial solvency and stability. Her expertise provides common sense, practical solutions, and hope for school leaders. Cindy serves with ACSI as the Vice President of Flourishing Initiatives, and has previously held roles at ACSI as the Director of Professional Development and Northeast Regional Director. In her current role, she oversees a number of ACSI teams working to support Christian schools' flourishing, including accreditation, professional development, certification, and assessment.

Dr. Roger C.S. Erdvig has served as head of school at Wilmington Christian School (Delaware) and Smithtown Christian School (New York), where he led initiatives to re-frame a commitment to distinctively Christian teaching and learning. In 2023, Roger is transitioning from local school leadership to serve as the Director of Worldview Education with Summit Ministries in Colorado. Writing and speaking as a Summit team member, Roger will build on the momentum from his book, *Beyond Biblical Integration*, which has helped thousands of Christian school leaders and teachers immerse students in a biblical worldview in every course, subject, and school activity.

Dr. Mitch Evans has over twenty years of teaching experience in Kingdom education schools. He currently serves as a high school AP Biology teacher at North Raleigh Christian Academy (North Carolina) and as an instructor in Liberty University's School of Education doctoral program. He holds a degree in microbiology and cell science from The University of Florida and earned his Doctor of Education from Southeastern Baptist Theological Seminary, where he studied the relationship between biblical worldview and Christian education.

Kim Fullerton is the Academic Dean for the Upper School at Little Rock Christian Academy (LRCA) in Arkansas. With more than twenty years of experience teaching Spanish, English, and biblical worldview, along with writing curriculum, designing courses, and mentoring teachers, Kim has contributed in varied ways to the growth and development of the LRCA high school. Working in a wide array of administrative roles has paved the way for her current role at LRCA. She holds a bachelor's degree in Spanish and a master's degree in English from the University of Central Arkansas.

Dr. Annie Gallagher, the founder of Transformed PD, is a professional development coach and instructional program consultant who currently lives in Kentucky. She has coached Christian educators and instructional leaders in the U.S. and internationally in how to authentically plan and teach Christ-centered instruction, so students see God revealed in content area subject matter. Dr. Gallagher is primarily known for coaching teachers through the PAQ (Purpose, Assumptions, Questions) method of providing Christ-centered instruction, which she developed as part of her doctoral research at Columbia International University and which was supported by Summit Ministries.

Dr. Matthew H. Lee is Director of Research at the Association of Christian Schools International (ACSI). He is co-editor of *Religious Liberty and Education* (Rowman & Littlefield, 2020), co-author of *Future Ready* (ACSI & Cardus, 2022), and author of numerous peer-reviewed research articles, book chapters, technical reports, and op-eds on civics education, education leadership, and religious education. At ACSI he leads research efforts examining school culture, spiritual formation, and education policy.

Dr. Debbie MacCullough has taught at the elementary, middle, high school, and university level for over thirty years in both the U.S. and the Philippines. A graduate of Cairn University (BS in Bible, BS in Education), Arcadia University (MA in Mathematics Education) and Penn State University (Ph.D. in Curriculum and Instruction), she has studied education and how to train others to teach. She loves teaching mathematics, particularly to those who do not find mathematics easy, as well as refining how to train others to help students think from a biblical worldview. Currently, Debbie works with the Association of Christian Schools International (ACSI) as Director of Global Core Standards. It is her desire to see education that is authentically Christian expand and improve.

Jerry Nelson is the Chief Ministry Officer at the Association of Christian Schools International (ACSI). He oversees all initiatives related to spiritual formation, focused on the elevation of God's Word, prayer, biblical worldview development, and the fulfillment of the Great Commission for all of ACSI's stakeholders, programs, and content. Jerry served on the ACSI Board before joining the staff, as well as head of school at Northwest Christian Academy in Miami for eleven years. He holds a bachelor's degree in History and a master's degree in Educational Leadership from St. Thomas University in Miami.

Eric W. Price is Research Associate at the Association of Christian Schools International. Previously, he worked at Georgetown University's Center on education and the workforce, where his research focused on economic and industry sector analysis, postsecondary education reform, and occupational personality. Eric holds a Masters of Public Policy from Georgetown University's McCourt School of Public Policy and a Bachelors in Economics from Rollins College.

Dr. Justin Smith is the Assistant Head of School at Little Rock Christian Academy (LRCA) in Arkansas, where he has led in administration, teaching, and coaching. A graduate of the University of San Diego, he earned his doctorate in Educational Leadership from Sam Houston State. With a number of published articles, chapters, and peer-reviewed presentations on record, he also received the Excellence in Superintendency Program Award from Sam Houston State University and recognition as The Woodlands Preparatory School's Most Inspirational Educator. Dr. Smith did his post-graduate work at the Harvard Graduate School of Education and is currently enrolled at the Saïd Business School at the University of Oxford earning a Diploma in Organizational Leadership.

Dr. Larry Taylor is the president of the Association of Christian Schools International (ACSI). He previously spent twenty years as the head of school at Prestonwood Christian Academy (PCA) in Plano, Texas, during which time Dr. Taylor co-launched a national training institute for schools, "Becoming a Kingdom School Institute," and developed a training program for parents titled "Becoming a Kingdom Family." Dr. Taylor authored the book *Running with the Horses* (WestBow Press, 2013), which helps parents raise children to be servant leaders for Christ and helps to build a family plan.

ABOUT THE SERIES EDITOR

Dr. Lynn E. Swaner is the Chief Strategy and Innovation Officer at ACSI, where she leads initiatives and develops strategies to address compelling questions and challenges facing Christian education. Dr. Swaner serves as a Cardus Senior Fellow and is the co-author or editor of multiple books on Christian education, including *Future Ready: Innovative Missions and Models in Christian Education* (ACSI & Cardus, 2022), *Flourishing Together: A Christian Vision for Students, Educators, and Schools* (Eerdmans, 2021), and *MindShift: Catalyzing Change in Christian Education* (ACSI, 2019). Prior to joining ACSI, she served as a professor of education and a Christian school administrator in New York.

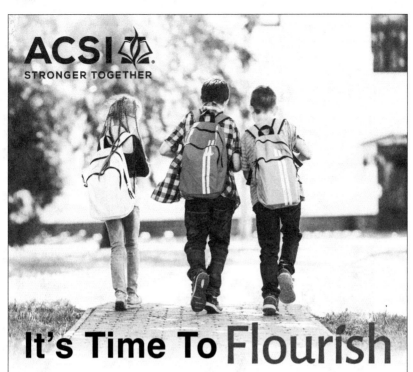

It's Time To Flourish

Think for a moment: In 100 years, what legacy do you want to leave for the students who sat in your classrooms? ACSI wants to come alongside you and help your school community flourish how God intends—biblically.

ACSI has been leading Christ-centered education toward excellence for more than 40 years, always seeking to understand what truly impacts and improves a Christian school. Through a multiyear endeavor, ACSI Research identified thirty-five constructs that support five primary domains of flourishing, which contribute to a school community marked by healthy spiritual, emotional, and cultural characteristics. This research was validated by a rigorous independent review and has blossomed into the ACSI Flourishing Initiative, which aligns ACSI Research, Professional Development, and Accreditation with a focus on flourishing students, educators, and Christian schools.

ACSI *Leading Insights: Special Education* advances Christ-centered education by focusing on schools' responsiveness to special needs, which is a validated construct in the flourishing domain of Expertise & Resources.

To learn more, please visit acsi.org/flourishing.

More from Leading Insights